www.hackingsales.com

What Others Are Saying About Hacking Sales

"Companies that embrace technology and data in their sales process will build the world class sales organizations that win. Hacking Sales creates an actionable, cutting edge sales process that can scale with your sales org and the ever changing world of technology."

-**Mark Roberge**, Chief Revenue Officer at Hubspot

"Max's sorted through the maelstrom of sales & marketing apps out there to cut through the clutter and show us some creative & practical ways to automate sales drudgery. Well done sir!"

-**Aaron Ross**, Built Outbound Sales at Salesforce. Co-founder of Predictable Revenue and Carb.io

"Hacking Sales succinctly shows sellers how to use new technology and sales tactics to up their game."

-**Elay Cohen**, Former SVP of Sales Productivity at Salesforce. Co-founder and CEO of SalesHood

"Max has become a dominant force in the next wave of sales: the use of technology, training, and best practices to turn sales into a true science. Sales can truly now be hacked much in the way we learned in the last generation to hack marketing into a quantitative growth engine. Hacking Sales has uniquely captured these changes, bringing together sales thought leadership and leading next generation technologies to together quantify and scale sales dramatically faster than ever before. Kudos, and thank you, to Max."

-**Jason Lemkin**, Co-founder and ex-CEO at Echosign. Founder at SaaStr. Managing Director at Storm Ventures

"Traditional sales methods have not kept pace with how customers want to buy today. Sales technology is finally catching up to the market and Max has created the ultimate playbook on how to sell in this era of Sales Acceleration."

-**Gary Swart**, Former CEO of oDesk. Partner at Polaris Partners

2

"Max is at the forefront of this new age of selling and has done a fantastic job in this book outlining the process of building and evolving a sales approach and process with tools, tips and techniques along the way. I recommend it to any Sales rep or Sales leader who is looking to play catch up or stay ahead of this ever-evolving profession we call Sales."

-**John Barrows**, Leading Sales Trainer for Salesforce, LinkedIn, Zendesk, Marketo, Box, and many of world's top tech sales organizations

"Max has packed this book full of actionable advice that will allow any sales professional to cut through the clutter and immediately improve results, by using proven techniques and tools. If you are an individual contributor or early stage founder looking to accelerate growth, reading this book will be the highest ROI you will get from your time today."

-**Matt Cameron**, Former Global Head of Corporate Sales at Yammer. VP of Sales at Kahuna

"One lesson I learned early in my career is to never be satisfied. Whether you're the #1 sales rep at your company, recently received a promotion into management, or are the CEO of Fortune 500 company you can always be pushing harder and performing better. Hacking Sales is an education in the new era of sales that will help sales orgs grow and innovate in ways they didn't know they could."

-**Sam Blond**, VP of Sales at Zenefits, the fastest growing SaaS company in history

"Sales is undergoing such a major transformation; some would say so much that the profession may be at risk. Max has responded by starting a movement where sales professionals can share and learn from each other regularly through thought leadership, events, community and networking. This book is a critical must-have component to anyone who wants to stay ahead of this transformation."

-**Emmanuelle Skala,** VP of Sales at Influitive

"Finally! A single, consolidated playbook to help start-ups define their prospecting strategy and sales philosophy. Max breaks down the areas to consider and the tools to evaluate in helping you maximize your resources. A great read for any VP Sales who's building their team out."

-**Bill Binch**, VP of World Wide Sales at Marketo

"Max Altschuler and the Sales Hacker team are always on point. They remain at the forefront of knowing what's hip, what's now, and what's driving revenue for today's sales organizations. The tools and technologies explored in this book will bring you to the front of the line - on your sales team, in your industry, and at your bank." - Ralph Barsi, Sales Development leader, Achievers

-**Ralph Barsi**, Director of Sales Development at Achievers

"Over the last few years, the sales development field has strongly emerged as the biggest innovation to happen to the sales process. There are not many who are more educated on this than Max Altschuler. Max shares his insights here as one of the only real references you'll need to understand this emerging space. After a quick read, you'll be able to boost revenue for your business and double down on your knowledge of modern day selling."

-**Kyle Porter**, Co-founder and CEO of SalesLoft

"Max has spent the last 3 years not only working in the trenches of B2B sales teams, he's also networked and collaborated with the most talented practitioners as part of his growing Sales Hacker movement. In this book, he has been gracious enough to share truly actionable strategies that just don't get written about it traditional cookie cutter sales books. For both sales leaders and salespeople, this is a must read."

-**Tawheed Kader**, Founder and CEO of ToutApp

"I've been lucky to have a first row seat watching Max create a new school of sales over the past few years. His real world experience, constant optimization, and questioning of traditional sales norms has created the best practices in this book that are essential for any sales team."

-**Jaspar Weir**, Co-founder and President at TaskUs

"Hacking Sales is the definitive guide to building a powerful sales machine that leverages the wide range of technology and data available today. Max has delivered a gift to sales reps and managers everywhere."

-**Ryan Buckley**, Co-founder and Head of Sales at Scripted

As sales becomes more scientific, sales teams need to stay up to date on all the new technologies and processes. Max Altschuler knows them all!

-**Armando Mann**, VP of Sales at RelateIQ

Max is one of the original hackers and like all hackers he's full of tips and tricks for you to follow and swallow to master the game of sales. It doesn't matter how much experience you have selling, you will most certainly gain some new knowledge by reading this book. It is chock full of unique ideas and approaches for you to use. This is a must read for anyone just getting into sales.

-**Doug Landis**, VP of Sales Productivity at Box

Author's Note

The companies mentioned in this book are not in any way affiliated with Sales Hacker, Inc. I do not work for, invest in, or get paid by any of these companies. The companies listed are in no particular rank or order. I provide information and my opinion, but it's up to the reader to decide which companies to do business with and what process to follow.

Visit HackingSales.com for more info and bonus material.

Contents

Introduction

Why Sales, Why Now?

The world of sales is blowing up. It's a $500 billion dollar industry that employs over 15 million people in the US alone. Salesforce, a sales technology company, may soon be doing $10 billion in ARR. For reference, that's what the NFL made in revenue in 2014.

Sales itself is undergoing a transformation. One could call it the acceleration or automation era. There is more financial investment in sales, and more talented people are choosing careers in sales than ever before. The Ivy Leaguers that would once jump straight to finance jobs at Goldman Sachs are getting into the sales game instead. Big venture capital firms are funding sales automation and acceleration start-ups. There are more cash-rich companies in the space with capital to spend on natural acquisitions than ever before. It's a good time to be in sales.

Business executives are realizing that a good sales team will make or break your business. Here's a quote from Peter Thiel's lecture on distribution, given in his Stanford computer science class. Peter is one of Silicon Valley's most outspoken angel investors.

> *The first thing to do is to dispel the belief that the best product always wins. There is a rich history of instances where the best product did not, in fact, win. Nikola Tesla invented the alternating current electrical supply system. It was, for a variety of reasons, technologically*

better than the direct current system that Thomas Edison developed. Tesla was the better scientist. But Edison was the better businessman, and he went on to start GE. Interestingly, Tesla later developed the idea of radio transmission. But Marconi took it from him and then won the Nobel Prize. Inspiration isn't all that counts. The best product may not win.

–Peter Thiel *CS183 - Class 9*

That's from someone who's been a part of some of the most successful tech companies of the past two decades (PayPal, Facebook, Yelp, Palantir, and many more), is worth over $2 billion, and comes from a product background.

Sales is in everything you do. If you still don't think it's an important skill, just look at anyone who's ever been President of the United States—or anyone who's ever been a politician in general. They are all true salesmen at heart.

Yet with all of these facts, only a handful of colleges offer degrees in sales and most MBA programs don't offer a single sales class. That's why I'm writing this book.

So much is changing, and there are so many new things to take advantage of as a modern-day salesperson. So today, consider this your enrollment—the beginning of your degree in modern sales. I call it Sales Hacking.

Who This Book Is For

This book was written for anyone who is in a selling role. To be more specific, this book is for:

- The individual reps who want to get ahead of their peers and be at the top of their organization
- The early sales hire that has to sell and create a process as he goes
- The early-stage company with a co-founding team looking to build out a sales process that they can then bring in experienced salespeople to run
- Anyone building a sales process in which you sell to an entity, such as business, government, and so on.

Where This Book Fits In

- Your company has a sales process, but it was built in the Prohibition Era.
- You have a process and you're crushing it, but you're working too hard.
- You have product market fit, and some paying customers—Now what?

What This Book Is Not

- Start-up Sales 101. I am not here to help you get product market fit, validate ideas, give you lean start-up methodology, etc. Want more of this? **Steli Efti** has a great short book on this that I recommend.
- The answer to all of your problems. You're still going to have to figure out what works for your individual business. Every one of them is different. I *can* give you the guidance you need to figure those things out on your own though, and that's extremely valuable.
- A guide on how to hire, train, and manage teams. I'm here to help the sellers, hunters, and deal-closers.

Having a process, even if it's weak, is extremely important. Without it you're disorganized and disjointed. If you're not tracking and measuring, then how are you supposed to get better? A process is *always* a work-in-progress, no matter how good the results. The best assets of sales teams and salespeople are great organizational and analytical skills. Companies that figure this out early, and build a strong and streamlined engine, will surpass their competitors. Reps that figure this out will out-sell their peers.

This book was made to help you build a strong foundation. Specifically, this book will help you to do the following:

- Build pipeline in a repeatable and scalable manner that can be refined and enhanced over time
- Close deals faster and nurture leads properly
- Take advantage of all of the new technologies that make it possible to be more efficient

This book can be used at any stage of a B2B business. Some companies will use this book later on to strengthen an existing business. Some will use it early and build from scratch. Consider this your guidebook.

A lot of books claim to have all of the answers, but that's ridiculous. In the end, all companies are made differently. Different variables such as industry, country, deal size, deal cycle, and target buyers affect outcomes greatly.

While I don't promise to serve you the answers on a silver platter, I will put you on the path to find them for your company. I'll talk about problems and solutions as generally as possible, just know that parts of the process vary greatly for different companies. One example is Salesloft's cadence, which I'll explain later in the book, this cadence may be drastically different from what yours should be for many reasons. What they do may not work for you. Take this book as a guide, but don't blindly follow. Always test and optimize to find what's right for you.

Most of the book will focus on outbound sales. However, much of this advice will work for inbound sales as well, for example segmenting, messaging, and lead research are relevant to both.

Regardless of how much inbound you have, you should be doing some level of outbound. Always hunt. If your inbound is good you'll have cash to pay the base salary for an outbound hunter. If people come to you and want your services, others that haven't found you might show the same interest, right? Go upstream, aim high, and go get them!

Visit HackingSales.com at any time for more resources and bonus material on each section.

Chapter 1: Developing Your Sales Stack

Where Do I Start?

First, you need to understand the process from a bird's-eye view. A sales process is a repeatable and scalable system in which you engage potential buyers and facilitate them through the stages of your pipeline. This process runs from the top of the funnel down to the hand-off after they've signed the contract. There's a ton that goes into this pipeline development, which I'll get into shortly.

Two things to ask yourself are: What stages of the pipeline matter most to you? What are the milestones you'd like to hit along the way? Don't make too many stages as it can get confusing as you scale.

It might look something like this:

CONTACTED > QUALIFIED > DEMO > PROPOSAL > CLOSED

I recommend that each stage have its own checklist. For example, in the "Close" stage, make sure you ask for referrals.

The main things that matter when managing a pipeline are:

- Total number of deals in the pipeline
- Average deal size
- Percent of deals that move from stage to stage until close
- Average time a deal stays in the pipeline

You'll want to find baseline numbers to measure each stage of the sales process. Be extremely diligent about staying on top of these numbers as deals move from stage to stage. Using a good Customer Relationship Management (CRM) tool should help you to keep tabs on the health of your pipeline. I suggest a few CRMs later in this book.

At the end of the day, it all starts with leads. This is why outbound along with a good lead generation/prospecting process, is so important.

- More leads at the top of the funnel will result in better numbers at the bottom.
- Targeted leads at the top of the funnel result in better, faster results. These target leads are also known as your low-hanging fruit.

Aaron Ross, who created the outbound sales model at Salesforce, talks about the various lead types in his highly recommended and bestselling book, **Predictable Revenue**. He breaks down theses leads into three categories: Seeds, Nets, and Spears.

To quote Aaron,

- ***Seeds*** *are word-of-mouth leads, usually from prior relationships or happy customers. These are how companies get started and where most of your first customers come from.*
  - o ***Pros:*** *Highly profitable, word-of-mouth leads are the fastest to close and have the highest win rates. There's nothing better!*
  - o ***Cons:*** *It's almost impossible to proactively grow them. You just have to do your best and be patient.*

- **Nets** *are your marketing leads, such as internet marketing, events, webinars, white papers, advertising, and the like. You're casting a wide net, so this is about quantity over quality.*
  - **Pros:** *Easy to generate. Some kinds of marketing programs are scalable, you can generate leads from everlasting content, and they are highly measurable. There are ways to generate leads at almost no cost.*
  - **Cons:** *Not sure what will work, most leads aren't a fit, low conversion rates, mostly individuals / small businesses, small order sizes, a lot of cost and effort to build, optimize, and maintain.*
- **Spears** *are when you have salespeople or business development people reaching out to specific targets, lists, or kinds of companies. It's a specific, targeted approach, driven by a human, with a goal of quality over quantity (the reverse of marketing Nets).... To be effective and scalable, you need a team of dedicated reps who only prospect— they don't close, manage accounts, or respond to inbound leads.*
  - **Pros:** *Very predictable results, enables a very targeted approach to ideal prospects at executive levels, fast is-it-working-or-not feedback cycle, creates a pool of sales talent.*
  - **Cons:** *Not profitable for small deals or customers, hard for old school companies to get the culture right (must avoid boiler room mentality), may be hard to get executive commitment to specialize and hire dedicated prospectors.*

Good leads are a good start, but then it's all about how you guide them through your pipeline. Consider a streamlined process, which will act as lubrication for your pipeline. This lubrication consists of automation and acceleration tools, outsourced help, and all sorts of tactical and strategic sales hacks to speed things up.

A good sales process is science, and science is the new art.

What's Your Sales Stack?

Developers and marketers have had their stacks for years. Developers have had the benefit of being able to build their own, and marketing has been fairly technical for a while now. Finally today there are enough sales tools for salespeople to build their own stack of technology.

The great thing about these new tools is that they connect in various ways. I use a series of API integrations, manual virtual assistant work, and spreadsheets to piece it together. You can think of your stack as your sales tool belt.

Here's what a sales stack can look like:

SALES STACK

SCRAPING LISTS

CONTACT INFO

OUTBOUND EMAIL

CRM

LEAD RESEARCH

DEMOS

PROPOSALS

CONTRACT

Now, there are many different ways to build a sales stack, and plenty of tools you can take advantage of for each piece. Some of the tools I'll mention in this book do very similar things, and you don't have to use just one. I use multiple e-mail grabbing tools in my sales stack.

I recommend finding the best subset of tools for your business, and making sure to be diligent about connecting them properly. You can try out integration tools like Zapier, IFTTT, or Bedrock Data if you need help. The less you have to do manually, the more efficient you will be.

"In a modern sales organization, leads and lead data span multiple applications. Being able to properly integrate the tools used to work a sales pipeline from start to finish is a must."
                                        –Wade Foster, CEO of Zapier

At the end of the day, you can have all of the technology in the world, but if you don't know how to use it you're not going to get very far.

Okay, now that we've got that out of the way, let's get into the good stuff.

Chapter 2: List Building – Part 1: Where Are Your Customers?

Finding Your Ideal Customer Profile

Building strong lists to generate leads at the top of the funnel is arguably the most important piece of your process. Without leads or nets, as Aaron Ross calls them, you have nothing. So start where your customers are. This is also called finding your ideal customer profile.

Here are a few questions you might want to ask yourself to jump-start this process:

- What products are my customers using that I compete with, complement, or might translate to interest in my product?
  - E.g. If you have a Mailchimp-style service, you want to speak to Mailchimp customers.
  - E.g. If potential customers are running Facebook Ads, they might also be interested in Ad Optimization or Analytics software.

- Where are these people living on the web?
  - E.g. Someone interested in your E-commerce service might have a store hosted on Shopify or built with Magento.
  - Eg.. If you want to find people to create courses online, go find people who have already created content on the subject in book form and are selling it on Amazon. Then convince them to try video content.

- What do I consider my low-hanging fruit?

- These are the people already doing what you want them to do, just somewhere else.
- E.g. Someone buying or selling a service on Craigslist that your company provides. It's easier to get the person to use you over Craigslist than to create a new buyer/seller from scratch. Pinterest has emerged as another way to source potential customers that are already playing ball.
- E.g. You're going after their budget focused on ad-spend and you see that a potential buyer has a testimonial on a competing company's website. You know they have budget and are already spending it somewhere else. Time to go get your slice or even the whole pie!

- What can I decipher from my previous closed deals that I can use in new ones?
  - You keep closing deals with companies, so take a moment to ask yourself, what do these companies have in common and how can I apply this when speaking to companies with the same common variables?

Some good places to look for information about potential buyers are:

- LinkedIn and Facebook groups
- Meetup
- Industry conference websites
- Trade association forums and directories
- Job boards like Indeed, LinkedIn, etc.
- Public Legal Fillings
- CrunchBase
- AngelList

- Glassdoor
- Yelp
- Shopify
- Etsy
- Kickstarter
- Any company database or marketplace

Once you have this information down, you finally know where to start looking for leads. We're going to start with getting company information first.

Easy, Non-Technical Web Scraping

Two pieces of software I like to use for scraping lists off the internet are Import.io and Kimono Labs. Since I am not a developer, I need to take advantage of tools that allow me to scrape without using any code and that's what these tools do. If you have a developer on staff with some free time (but get real, how often does that happen?), by all means, have him build you a scraper with more functionality. For most sales hackers, either of these tools is all you need.

Kimono Labs

Kimono can be used in the lead generation stage of the sales process, enabling reps to build massive lists of leads and collect e-mails or names of potential leads by crawling various websites, such as marketplaces or company websites.

Pratap Ranade, Kimono Labs CEO, says:
> The problem is that useful data on the web is (a) scattered across websites and is semi-structured or unstructured, (b) this data changes sporadically, (c) it is

not available programmatically. Kimono enables anyone (developers and non-developers) to turn websites into structured APIs (updated feeds of structured data), enabling users to collect data at scale, keep it up to date and use it to automate their workflows with very little effort.

Reps can use Kimono with full contact to collect more information about a particular lead based on his or her e-mail address, then use mail merge products to send canned e-mails to the list. Reps and managers also use Kimono to feed updated data into the CRM.

Justin Wilcox of Customer Development Labs uses Kimono and Streak to get e-mail addresses and reach out to large numbers of leads with effective cold e-mails.

Import.io

Import.io also sits right at the beginning of the sales process when you're generating mass amounts of leads. It is important that, as an organization, you have product market fit and that your sales or marketing team can clearly articulate what a target customer looks like, so they can know where to find information about these people or organizations on the web.

Import.io is general platform for accessing data on the web. It was not specifically designed for lead generation. Nevertheless, advanced sales and marketing people discovered the technology, started using it for lead generation, and began writing about the success that they were having. Lead generation is a perfect use of the technology.

For simply getting data into an ordered, usable format, Google Sheets is a great tool to use in conjunction with Import.io. In addition, data extracted from the web using Import.io can also be imported into Salesforce or any other lead management or sales pipeline software.

Import.io Use Case:

Andrew Fogg, Chief Data Officer at Import.io. explains how to use the software:

This approach was developed by some of Import.io's earliest users, and it is both ingenious and simple:

1. *Find a website where your ideal user can be found.*
2. *Build an API to that website (using Import.io, naturally) and extract as much data about each lead as you can.*
3. *Pull that data into a spreadsheet.*

That's it. Three simple steps and it takes about 10 minutes, after which you will have thousands of quality leads to work with.

Now let's look at each of those steps in a bit more detail. To help you visualize how this can work for your business, I'm going to walk you through an example. Let's imagine that I'm in commercial real estate and want to talk to real estate brokers.

Step 1: Find your ideal user

The first step will require a little bit of imagination and thinking on your part. Where your ideal user can be found of course depends on who that person is. You'll probably need to spend some time getting to know your users and looking around the web to see where they hang out. Is it a forum? A professional association? Are they on social media?

The key here is to be as specific as possible when defining your ideal user (lead). The more specific you are, the more targeted your messaging can be. In our real estate example, I am going to use a real estate listing site in New York City. If I click through to one of those properties I can see the broker's name, e-mail (as a link from his name), and phone number—that's the data I'm after!

Step 2 & 3: Extract the data and get it in a spreadsheet

I've combined steps 2 and 3 together here, because they are closely tied to the same process.

To get this data I could use a number of different options. The simplest way to do this is to build a **Crawler**, which will then go to each part of the site and pull data from all the pages that match the ones I train it on. This means I will end up with a big list of names and contact information, which I can export into Excel, CSV or Google Sheets.

That's great, but Crawlers only create static data sets, which means that to get new data from this site I would have to re-crawl the whole site—and that would take a while. Instead, I can do something a tad more complicated by building an **Extractor** to one page. Then I use the URL pattern of that page to generate all the other URLs for that site and use this batch search

Google Sheet to pass all of those URLs through the Extractor. This has the benefit of being able to quickly refresh whenever I need to.

A quick note about getting the e-mail addresses: you'll notice, if you visit the page, that the e-mail address is displayed as a link to the estate agent's name. When I map this data, I need to make sure I map it as a link. It may look like I've only mapped his name, but when I export the data into Excel or Google Sheets, I will get one column with his name and another column with the text of the link—in this case his e-mail address.

In this particular example, I would also need to do a bit of data cleansing, because many of the properties are being sold by the same real estate agent so I am likely to end up with a lot of duplicates. This is easily done in either Excel/Google Sheets or most mass e-mailing software like MailChimp.

Now, sometimes these tools will only help you get a portion of the lists you need built, but they're a good start. This information can springboard you into getting the rest of the list built quickly using the tools in the next chapters. If you don't get contact information, like in the previous real estate example, you'll be able to use the information you do get to find the rest of the information later on.

Deeper Insights On Your Competitor's Customers

These services make it really easy for you to go after buyers that are already using competing or complementary products. For example, if Mailchimp users fit in to your Ideal Customer Profile, then you should use one of these services to go after those customers. It's up to you to turn them into new customers.

Datanyze

Datanyze fits into the first half of the sales cycle by helping sales development reps book more opportunities. Using the platform, reps can uncover new high-potential companies to reach out to, find the right contacts, and get their e-mail addresses, all in one shot.

Outside of sales prospecting, a lot of companies use Datanyze to retain their own customers. Customer success teams can get notified the day one of their customers has added a competitor's technology. This enables them to reach out to that customer before it's too late.

Datanyze integrates with Salesforce and syncs their technology and company data with any or all lead, account, contact, and opportunity records. This helps reps quickly identify which prospects are worth reaching out to right within their Salesforce account.

Ilya Semin, CEO of Datanyze says,
> *Personalization is everything when doing outreach. Don't just reach out to a prospect that uses a competitor and say you have a similar product. Address your key differentiators and show them that you're willing to go the extra mile to get their attention.*

Datanyze Use Case

KISSmetrics' sales reps use Datanyze Alerts to receive a daily summary of every website that has dropped a competitor's technology or added a technology that integrates with KISSmetrics. This enables them to get in touch with prospects that have a high potential to purchase their product. These are key buying signals that allow the reps to act quickly.

BuiltWith

BuiltWith allows you to see all websites that are using certain web-based services or integrations so you can easily create lead lists with the information.

Start creating your lead list by choosing the technology you're interested in. BuiltWith will come back with a list of all the sites on the internet using your chosen technology.

You can then customize your list by sorting and filtering as much as you need. The options for filtering your list include (but are not limited to):

- Location—down to postcode/ZIP
- Traffic Ranking
- People—names and titles of people at the business
- Company Names
- Vertical—shopping/forums/software
- Top Level Domains (TLD)—.com .uk .de
- Telephone numbers
- E-mail addresses
- Other technologies—find websites in your lead list that are using particular premium technologies

BuiltWith also allows you to get actual names, titles, and e-mails of people at companies. They claim to have seven plus years of historical data, and they've built a comprehensive contact and e-mail list providing users with the ability to see qualified e-mails for businesses where they've found titles and have known e-mail addresses for the company.

If you sign up for a paid plan, BuiltWith will pass their technology data into your Salesforce account so you can further qualify your leads.

BuiltWith Use Case

J. Ryan Williams leads the SDR team at Adroll and was one of their first sales reps back in 2011. An integral part of their sales growth was due to their clever use of BuiltWith's services. Adroll knew their Ideal Customer Profile was e-commerce stores, so J. Ryan used BuiltWith to tell him which sites were built using Magento. Magento is an e-commerce software platform that allows shop owners to quickly build a store online.

Other options to check out are iDataLabs, **Mixrank** and **SimilarWeb**.

Targeting Key Executives, Influencers, and High-Potential Buyers

In some cases you'll want to find an individual key player to target. Try these options to target based on social media and add them to your lists.

Followerwonk

Followerwonk is a social analytics tool for Twitter. It has many features, but one of the most popular use cases for business is "audience targeting."

By analyzing the top followers of any brand, or even your competitors, you can find highly qualified prospects, leads, or engagement opportunities. Followerwonk calculates the "Social Authority" of each Twitter account, so you can sort by the most influential people in each space.

Followerwonk Use Case

At Udemy they use Followerwonk to target people with certain words in their bios. If we wanted to find PHP experts to teach a programming course, we could use the bio search function to search Twitter bios for PHP. It was a great way for us to engage with and understand the players in the space. The best part was that we could sort by the number of followers they had and go after the ones with the biggest reach. Getting content on board was a win, but getting someone with a pre-existing audience was an even bigger win, as they would likely promote to that audience and turn them into Udemy students.

Little Bird

Little Bird helps you find influencers using certain keywords, see which potential buyers to connect with, and see who's connecting with your competitors. Similar to Followerwonk, you can easily use Little Bird to search Twitter for potential buyers based on criteria you create, such as company, location, follow-count, keywords, etc.

Little Bird can actually be used in many stages of the sales process. It can be used in the Lead Research phase when preparing for a sales call. Maybe you'd like to understand a business's ecosystem and the people who influence it. The Little Bird team itself uses the product to identify the people, publications, and business that matter to understand the space/players better on their initial discovery call. With this data in hand they have been able to qualify twice as many leads into sales opportunities.

Little Bird can also be used in the Lead Nurturing stage. By using the share and engage feature you can monitor trends in the space and leverage the information before other people do. You'll be positioned as the expert, be more consultative in your sale, and take the competitive advantage in the deal.

With Little Bird's API, you can pull data out of existing CRM systems, push it into Little Bird, and identify the influencers that cross multiple customer and prospect databases. This helps you and your marketing organization prioritize your efforts on relationship building.

Chapter 3: List Building – Part 2: Targeting Your High-Potential Buyer

Company Databases

So now you've built your lists by finding out where your Ideal Customer Profiles (ICPs) live on the internet. The next step is to find relevant company information at scale, so you know which ones are worth reaching out to first or are worth reaching out to with a higher degree of personalization. You'll also use this to further segment your lists later on.

There are plenty of databases out there for you to use to inquire about these companies. Things to look for might include:

- Amount of money raised to date
- Timing of last round raised
- Employee head count
- New employees recently added
- Job titles and new titles added
- Company headquarters
- PR announcements, like product, funding, key hires, or partnerships
- Legal filings

This is also how you tell your whales from your fish and the difference between who is ready and who is not. Again, keep refining your ICP until you have a core audience or perfect profile. Low-hanging fruit can be your easy wide-open layups. You just need to know what they look like.

Let's get into some of your best options for company information databases.

CrunchBase and AngelList

These are your free and simple sources for the information you need on tech companies from Pre-Seed to Post-IPO/Exit. Both CrunchBase and AngelList have APIs you can use, which are good, but still somewhat limited as they don't want you to rip their entire databases. If you're somewhat technical in basic Ruby or Python, or think you can learn quickly, check out COO of Scripted, Ryan Buckley's blog posts on Scraping CrunchBase.

If you're not too technical, you can use the non-technical web scraping tools previously mentioned (Import.io and Kimono Labs), to scrape the information you require. Supplement this with virtual assistants and you'll have everything you need to start building massive lists in one shot.

Glassdoor is also a good place to get company data.

Mattermark

Mattermark is a way of sourcing, analyzing, and tracking private companies around the world. By using the wealth of data they have on companies; using proprietary information such as a "Growth Score" or "Mindshare Score," allows B2B sales professionals to identify more readily potential private companies they would like to do business with.

Mattermark provides a feed into any user's instance of Salesforce, giving them the ability to leverage the data in their CRM. You can connect your LinkedIn account to see how your first-level connections are connected to the people in the private companies you have called up on Mattermark. This is a great way of getting warm introductions to these private firms.

They also have an API feed that a number of Mattermark users leverage to populate other tools and platforms they may be using internally.

Spiderbook

Spiderbook helps identify prospects and leads, and sits pre-CRM. Outside of your normal use case of lead generation, Spiderbook can also identify companies that will partner with you in the sales process, who to use for references, and what your competitive landscape looks like.

Spiderbook worked with an Enterprise IT Asset Management company called Oomnitza, who have a small inside sales team of three people. Oomnitza tried Hoovers, but the data was junk, so they moved to prospecting on LinkedIn manually, which was their most successful process until that point, with 3% conversions to demos set up. Spiderbook took their seed information like current customers, partners, suppliers, and product profile and matched it with customers online, which generated highly targeted lists. Add in personalized messaging and they went from 3% to 27% conversions to demos set up. Obviously that increase in demos could lead to a massive increase in revenue with the same team and sales process.

Aman Naimat, the CEO of Spiderbook, says:

No matter how good the leads are that we generate, you still need a four- to eight-touch sales process that is efficient and personalized. Even the perfect lead will fail if you don't follow a rigorous process and don't utilize relevant content to personalize the messaging.

Top-Down and Bottom-Up Targeting

The next step is finding out who in the organization you'll need to target. If you're just starting off this is a bit harder. Some industries make it a no-brainer. Selling in the digital ad space? You probably can derive from the market that you'll need to talk to the VP/Head of Digital Marketing. Selling sponsorships to in-person events? You can probably aim directly for the Field Marketing Manager.

These are your ideal customer profiles. In the case where you can't immediately figure this out, you'll employ either Top-Down or Bottom-Up outreach.

Top-Down

Aim for the highest person on that side of the organization that you can find. If it's someone in Marketing you want to speak with, but you don't know who, then reach out to the VP of Marketing or the CMO. You should *very* briefly introduce your product or product area, and ask to be introduced to the appropriate person. Below is an example of such an e-mail.

Subject: Appropriate Person
Or Subject: Referral Request

Hi [First name],

I see you work at [company] and was wondering if you could put me in touch with the person responsible for [X product value].

Many thanks for your help,
[Your name]

That's it.

A last ditch effort can be made to reach out to the CEO, but I would start with the highest person on that individual silo within the company.

This tends to work for two reasons:

1. The person you are e-mailing is not responding to you, they're introducing you to someone who will. The work on their part is minimal. Make the e-mail super short and to the point—and the point is getting the introduction, not pitching the product.
2. When the recipient receives the introduction, it's coming from their boss. Usually if their boss tells them to do something, they'll do it. They won't even ask for context most of the time.

This tactic and email has been widely spread, so beware that it's losing its effectiveness. You'll need to find ways to be more creative when working the Top-Down approach.

Bottom-Up

If the organization is larger, you can come at it from a different angle. Lists are so easy to build these days that it's worth a couple templated e-mails. This approach only works if it's a product that would be used company-wide or with somewhat junior people, like software sales. If it's a product like Domo, made for the CEO, it's probably not going to work.

Start by targeting a few junior employees and selling them on the fact that they can be champions for the product. They'll out-perform their peers and when the bosses ask how, they can plug the product to the team as the fastest way to earn a raise or promotion.

Farlan Dowell, VP of Sales at Upsight, spoke about this at a recent Sales Hacker Series event. He calls this the act of "becoming a hero maker," meaning, make the internal champion a hero by being the guy who brings on the amazing new product and proves it out for the team.

You can think of Bottom-Up almost like entering a parasite that infects the rest of the organization. I've heard reps say things to their bosses like, "If the company doesn't pay for this, I'll come out of pocket and by a one seat license myself." In this case, the rep knows that it's helping him close deals, hit quota, and make more money. If it costs him $39 per-month out of pocket, it's definitely worth it.

If you can do a good job at flipping these champions, odds are you'll have the full attention of the right decision maker in no time. It's a lot easier to get these junior employees started on free trials than it is to get in immediately with the VP.

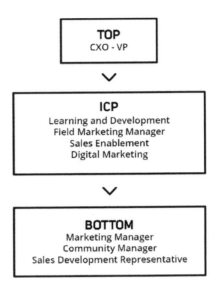

Lean on Your Industry Allies

Again, if you've already landed a few deals, this makes things a lot easier. My advice is to segment your past deals based on company size or deal size, and see if there are any common paths you've navigated within their organizational chart. Going through past deals allows you to figure out who you might have spoken to at a similar organization, and then gives you a potential job title to look out for at the new target company.

You can also reach out to or make friends at companies that are selling their products to similar companies, but are not your competitors.

Recently, I had the pleasure of meeting with the founder of VideoGenie, Justin Nassiri, and his first salesperson, Jake. They weren't sure who to target in their outreach to Fortune 1000 companies. They had no past data to look through, as these would be their first big accounts. I received an intro to them through the team at SocialChorus and recognized that they were selling to a similar market, but with very different and non-competing products. I simply recommended that the two teams share contacts for accounts, because it's a win-win-win. Don't be afraid to contact the peers in your industry to ask for help.

SellerCrowd

SellerCrowd is an anonymous forum that allows people in Ad Tech to exchange information to target companies and accounts. For example, if you're looking to sell digital media to Nike you can ask the forum who to speak to at Nike. You should get back a pretty informational response. You may even get contact information. We're still waiting for someone to do this for SaaS (Software as a Serivce)—could it be you?

LinkedIn Sales Navigator

I had a premium Sales Plus account and recently moved over to the Sales Navigator account. I use LinkedIn to get insights on company information, and then drill deep into job titles and employee backgrounds. For example, it's great to be able to quickly find the profiles of all employees that are Director-level, in Sales, have four plus years at the company, and are located in Dublin.

LinkedIn Sales Navigator finally gives you the LinkedIn user experience sales prospecting has been looking for. I have a team of virtual assistants that do my LinkedIn prospecting for me based on the direction I provide them, and this new format of lead searching should increase their numbers dramatically.

Another new feature is adding them to a leads list, as opposed to starring the contact as you would previously on LinkedIn. Once there, I can go back and InMail them, or export their e-mail using Datanyze or Saleloft, then contact them in multiple different ways over time.

LinkedIn is still the number one source for up-to-date information, so these new features go a long way in making it easier to search and sort through it all. I don't know why they didn't do it sooner. It's just one more step in LinkedIn's march to become your one and only CRM.

Using Twitter to Generate Warm Leads

Industry experts use the term "social selling" for when social media became big and salespeople who adjusted and embraced social became masters of generating new leads.

Well, now there's a new tool out there that automates most of this.

Socedo

Socedo allows you to pick conversations, keywords, hashtags, and handles to track prospects. Just set up prospect search criteria, Socedo selects accounts across Twitter that might be relevant to you, then you approve the prospects they've selected.

Once you have your list of prospects, Socedo favorites a recent tweet of theirs. An hour later they follow the prospect. When the prospect follows you back, they send a direct message using the prospect's first name, a reference to his or her tweet, and a CTA. This CTA is trackable and the entire flow, including the direct message, is customizable.

Socedo integrates directly with **Marketo** and **Salesforce** to track leads that are generated from social media further down the funnel. They also recommend using a social media management tool like **Buffer**, **HootSuite**, or **SproutSocial** to track conversations.

CEO of Socedo, Aseem Badshah, adds,

> *It's important to spend time coming up with some really good keywords that will help you find your target customers. Think about what they are tweeting about instead of what you or your competitors are tweeting about. What events do they attend? Who do they retweet? What do they read? The prospect search criteria takes some time, but it is crucial to your success no matter how you prospect.*

The team at Tallwave, for example, is using Socedo with an individual business development rep to look for start-up founders on Twitter, and then using the automated messaging to ask if the prospect would be interested in sharing more about their business. From there a call is set up and the rep can fill his day with qualified warm sales calls. They're setting up meetings this way more than through their outbound e-mail campaigns.

Visit HackingSales.com/Resources for more information on finding your Ideal Customer Profile and list building.

Chapter 4: Contact Information

Ok, now we're moving.

You have all of the information you could possibly need to build highly targeted lists of your potential buyers. You have potential targets at all levels within the companies, both ICP, top-down, and bottom-up. You have company names, job titles, and other attributes. The only thing you're missing now is their contact information, which is a really important piece of the puzzle.

Remove Duplicates Early On

Before you start getting contact information, you've probably built up quite a few lists from sources all over the Internet using the tactics from previous chapters in this book. That means you probably have a handful of duplicates on your lists. You don't want to go out collecting contact information while you still have duplicates, as you shouldn't waste time or resources getting e-mail addresses for the same person multiple times. Let's quickly remove duplicates from your lists.

My favorite way to do this is to use Google Sheets. They just released new Add-ons you can install easily from your Google Sheet.

Just click Add-ons in the navigation bar where File and Edit are, and find the Add-on called Remove Duplicates. Once you have that Add-on, put all of the sheets together on a master sheet. Then open Remove Duplicates and run the program to delete duplicate cells.

If your lists are already segmented and you want to keep them separate, create the master sheet and run the program, but don't allow it to delete duplicates. Instead, ask the program to highlight the duplicate and the original cells in green, then manually delete from one of the lists.

You also might want to check your current CRM for accounts that you're already talking to. The process for doing this is different with all CRMs, but you can usually pull a report, add it to the document, and remove duplicates (both from the original and from your CRM). You won't need to find the e-mail addresses if you already have them, so it should save you some time and money.

All of these minor, trainable tasks are perfect assignments for a virtual assistant to handle. I'll get to that in a bit.

Ok, now you're ready to generate contact information. There's no secret sauce as far as information goes. An e-mail address is number one. If you can get a direct phone number, that's good too.

Toofr

This is the best tool I've seen for building a massive list, as long as you can get a first name, last name, and domain name first. They can verify or find thousands of e-mails at a time. Just upload the .csv and then pull out the export file. This is big for lowering bounce rates, which can set off spam triggers and mess up the effectiveness of your e-mail campaigns.

For example, let's say my goal is to contact the VP of Marketing at 200 target companies that have just closed B round and are on CrunchBase. I can scrape the company information (first name, last name, domain) into a .csv using the tools from earlier in the book and upload that neatly organized .csv directly into Toofr. The final result should be a nice little .csv with verified e-mail addresses alongside the information I imported. The data comes from multiple sources and is usually double- or triple-verified, so it's pretty accurate.

According to the business development team at **Looker**, Toofr saves them between 30 and 40 hours of manual research every week depending on the number of people they are researching (normally about 1,000 per week).

Ryan Buckley, the CEO of Toofr, has some advice on getting the most out of your lists: "Get in a regular cadence with it. The most successful e-mail campaigns are honed over time. Test your subject lines and calls-to-action. Every list is different."

SalesLoft

SalesLoft is great for prospecting directly from LinkedIn, which means you have a target individual in mind and need his or her full contact information. I find this most helpful when I have a company and job title but I don't know the person's name that I'm looking for. Using LinkedIn's new Sales Navigator, I can now easily search LinkedIn for these contacts and simply export them using the SalesLoft Chrome extension. SalesLoft will show me my lists of exports and, to their best guess, the full contact information for my exported leads. SalesLoft's data is usually pretty accurate.

In the case that all you have is a company name and a desired job title it can still be a bit manual, but that's what you have virtual assistants for.

Capture (by RingLead)

Capture is a really neat new tool from RingLead that allows you to go to any site or social profile and pull data using a Chrome browser extension.

For example, you can visit a company team page and scrape all team member's names. This allows you to get their contact information and import it directly into Salesforce. The extension allows you to do this from websites, social profiles, job listing sites, spreadsheets, Twitter lists, Google searches, and more.

Capture can even be used within Salesforce to keep existing data up to date, or used with existing external databases to update incomplete or stale data.

Ecquire

Ecquire is another browser add-on that allows you to sync and find new leads in real-time. It can actually pull up leads by hovering on CrunchBase and AngelList as well as LinkedIn and Gmail. If you're using a CRM and want more functionality than Rapportive plus the ability to prospect via other channels, this is a great option.

Since they connect to your CRM, it tells you which contacts on the page are already in the system and which ones are new. It will also add new data for the contact if it's different in the CRM. It's a pretty intuitive piece of software.

Connectifier

Connectifier is one of my favorite new tools. It's another Chrome extension that I can use when looking at any social profile across the web. When you pull up the profile, a sidebar pops up with public and known e-mail addresses and phone numbers that are extremely accurate. Sometimes it can even get people's personal Gmail addresses.

It also provides direct links to other social profiles, such as Meetup, AngelList, and Quora in a way that is similar to Rapportive, but much more robust.

Anyreach

Anyreach allows you to pull all contact information directly off webpages. It's another way to scrape as much data as possible. All you do is plug in a domain using the full URL, (https://www.___.com) and click Go. It will pull all contact information from across the site as the internal crawler goes page by page. They also have a bulk upload tool and an API for those requiring multiple domain look-ups.

SellHack

SellHack is similar to Toofr in that you need to have some current information on your contact to get more information. This is best for individual e-mail look-ups on the go, which you get by using the nifty browser extension. It also has an API for bulk lookups.

The prospector tool that's in the works looks really interesting because it's similar to SalesLoft, but seems to be able to extract data on Github, Stack Overflow, Google+, and Twitter.

Lukewarm E-mailer

Lukewarm E-mailer allows you to scrape Twitter and pull data into a Google Spreadsheet. Then their team goes out to find e-mail addresses or contact information for each cell. It effectively turns Twitter into a lead engine. Try using it with Followerwonk or Little Bird.

Two other solid options for accurate individual e-mail look-ups are **Voila Norbert** and **E-mailBreaker.**

If you're in Ad Tech, try **SellerCrowd**, as mentioned earlier.

If you're in E-commerce check out **Pipetop**.

Have more money than time? You can always use a database like **Data.com**, **Hoovers**, or **ZoomInfo**. However, we found that the data can be stale or the contacts may be getting pounded with e-mails from everyone else using that same database of leads.

E-mail Verification and Enrichment

Now that you've built massive e-mail lists from various data sources, you might want to do two things quickly.

First, make sure the e-mails are verified and don't bounce. High bounce rates can lead to blacklisted domains, which will send your e-mails to people's spam folders. Bad e-mail addresses will also throw off your e-mail optimization efforts and screw up conversion funnel.

Second, enrich the data you have so you get a full lead profile you can work with. This gives you a quick and easy way to turn and email address into a full built out profile on the other person.

BriteVerify

BriteVerify is extremely simple and easy to use. Its service allows you to verify e-mails one-by-one or upload lists to verify multiple e-mails all at once.

Its API is the best part. It allows you to connect your CRM, POS software, web forms, or mobile applications so that any e-mail that comes in is automatically verified as soon as it's entered into your system.

Also check out new comer **Kickbox.io**.

Clearbit

Clearbit is a really easy-to-use enrichment tool with an API that you can pass a lead through, and it will tell you everything you need to know about that lead. You can pass numerous domain names or e-mail addresses through the API, and they'll fill out a full profile based on that information.

Clearbit is a really good way to clean up new data, fill in the blanks, or keep data clean.

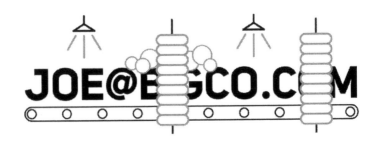

Chapter 5: Lead Research

List Building and Lead Research go hand and hand in the sales process. At this point, your lists are fully built, but are not yet ready to be put into action.

Why? Because you still need to learn things about your prospects so you can deliver a message relevant to them and provide value in the sales process. Better yet, you still need to know who you need to learn more about and segment these lists further. These are just two key reasons it's important to research and prepare ahead of time.

Now, there have been heated debates in many sales circles about the outbound sales process. Some people like to play a spray and pray game where you blast out e-mails, like the "appropriate person" e-mail I referred to in Chapter 3. Others like to show every prospect a certain level of personalization in the e-mail. Regardless of what you do, it all comes down to Lead Research, Segmenting, and Messaging.

We'll dive deep into Segmenting and Messaging in the next two chapters, but for now let's talk Lead Research.

You'll want to find out as much information as possible on the company and individual contacts before you reach out to important prospects. Find triggers or action events to use as a reason to contact them at this time.

Below are examples of trigger events.

Company

- Fundraise, liquidity event, acquisition, or company milestone
- New headquarters or expansion
- Key executive hire
- Good PR (company is growing, product release, CEO on *Ellen*, etc.)
- Good blog post
- Competitor PR
- Awards or recognition
- New contracts or partnerships

Individual

- Job change
- Awards or recognition (Field Marketing Manager after a successful Dreamforce event)
- Good blog post
- Twitter or social trigger event (you will know from their Twitter, if they care about a local sports team winning the Super Bowl, etc.)

> **Seller:** Hey John! Did you catch the big game yesterday?
>
> **Buyer:** Umm, it's Jen and yeah, we lost!
>
> *DO YOUR RESEARCH!*

The data is all over the Internet, but uncovering it is the hard part. The Internet can be a massive black hole, so you need a good way to sift through the noise to find relevant content about your prospect's company. Many of these companies solving this problem are using a mix of scraping, crawling, AI, and big data analysis.

Trigger Event, Alerts, and Researching

InsideView

InsideView is one of the most robust tools in the space, and it continues to go wider and deeper. It's a great tool for keeping your data up to date by tracking what's happening within accounts across the Internet. It allows you to sort through its prospect database to track, and even contact, companies with relevant trigger events.

They provide the rep with updates on all business and social events happening for each prospect. This consists of notifications and a daily e-mail alerts delivered right to your inbox. You can also get a real-time dossier on every prospect in your CRM, hence the "CRM intelligence."

You can even use it to figure out which connections in your network can introduce you to potential buyers who are on your list. This works through connected social networks and company's internal employee networks.

Gagein

Gagein relies on artificial intelligence to extract sales triggers from millions of sources, including media, social media, and—most importantly—company websites. This process not only identifies large company prospects, it also uncovers prospects among mid-size companies that other tools don't find.

For example, real estate companies or real estate

management services can find out about ownership shifts or new facilities before their competitors. Since Gagein tracks websites and not just news sources, it can alert vendors to key information before it becomes common knowledge. One customer used Gagein to find out who bought a factory that had just been up for sale on the day that the deal closed. The customer was able to contact the new owners before the story hit the news.

Richard Dym, CMO of Gagein, says,
Gagein was created to flip the odds of a deal in favor of the salesperson. Research tells us that if you are the first salesperson to call on a prospect, and can engage in a consultative manner, that you have a 74% chance of closing the deal. So it's all about knowing when and why to reach out. This is exactly what Gagein does.

FunnelFire

FunnelFire continuously tracks keywords across thousands of news sources. In normal use, this allows users to find relevant articles about industry topics to use in their sales process. Another way to use this data is to have FunnelFire identify companies mentioned in different ways and with different trigger events. Several customers use this data to help them identify new companies to target. When they combine this with alerts on trigger events, end users can be notified about new companies falling into particular trigger events and use this to find new leads.

A publicly traded company uses FunnelFire in several ways. On a daily basis, the marketing team gets massive amounts of inbound leads. These leads get pushed automatically into their CRM. The CRM auto-assigns the sales reps based on territory and a number of rules. Through the FunnelFire CRM integration, profiles on these new leads are generated on the fly. They are compiled from thousands of data sources and profiles across the web, and a dossier is created instantaneously so the sales rep can gather information and assess the company in seconds.

Mark LaRosa, CEO of FunnelFire, adds,
> *Most of the sales process has been completed by the time reps call on prospects. Prospects are more educated than ever, because data is everywhere. As a result, they expect sales reps to be just as educated.*

DiscoverOrg

DiscoverOrg is set apart by the fact that it employs a team that consistently dials into accounts to make sure their database information is fresh. They almost act as your pre-SDR, gathering company and market information, following trigger events and job changes, and figuring out org structure and contact information.

They integrate with many top CRMs and even offer a browser extension for real-time use.

Mention.io

Mention.io is one of the simplest ways to track mentions and keywords across the web. Many companies use it to track themselves, as it helps reduce online noise surrounding references to your brand. Salespeople who want a cheap and quick alternative to the more robust tools previously mentioned will find this to be a good solution.

LinkedIn Advanced Settings and Sales Navigator

LinkedIn Advanced Settings and Sales Navigator provide relevant content and news from your prospects, delivered to you in real time. This has worked well since their acquisition of Newsle, which had similar functionality.

If you're looking for something really basic, you can always go the **Google Alerts** route

Check out **Birdhouse** to get twitter alerts on your Contacts and Accounts.

Predictive Sales and Web Signaling

This is a really interesting new wrinkle in the mix. These companies are working on ways to take information from your past deals, your top keywords, public information, news, and other buying signals to create a web of potential buyers. This is the power of the new era in sales. Salespeople never would've been able to see these potential leads in that past. Developers are bringing their witchcraft to our playing fields, and it's just getting interesting. These tools allow you to see and capitalize on your lowest-hanging fruit.

Infer

Infer provides you with, what they call, predictive lead scoring. They integrate with your data via CRM or Marketing Automation software to develop a customized list of buying signals that they can then use to find companies looking to buy from you. All you need is an e-mail address or company name and Infer can build a robust buying profile for that lead.

They can also tell you which of your current marketing qualified leads (MQLs), you can consider more easily closable than other leads. They do this based on multiple factors that they gather from public information, such as recent news, company size, new job openings, social media use, legal filings, etc.

Infer also uses the data from your CRM and pairs it with machine learning, so that when you input a new lead they can give an accurate lead score based on past deal wins and losses.

Fliptop

Fliptop looks at your existing customers and previous wins and losses to determine what traits define success for your organization. Once they've identified signals and data points that make up your ICP, they can score leads in the system based on win probability.

Leads that come in from Inbound get a score right away. This section integrates with Marketo extremely well. The higher the score, the higher priority you should give those leads, for example by passing them on to your best rep or giving them a call immediately.

They can also take the leads you've imported into your CRM and score them, even if they've come from lead generation initiatives like the ones mentioned in this book. Their system will then uncover your low-hanging fruit.

Compile

Compile aggregates data from the deep public web including, among others, message board chatter, budget documents, security advisories, and news sites.

A natural language processor-based engine called the Autocurator sifts through the data to identify only those bits that indicate a potential sales opportunity. The engine identifies patterns that indicate a clear buying action.

For example, a technology roadmap presentation discussing a new citywide Wi-Fi network or a recent data breach at a global organization is a good indicator of a need for a specific product, and would show up publicly across the Internet.

Using a trained set of known good and known bad leads, the Autocurator assigns a score to each lead. Only those leads which display a clear buying trigger and strong relevance to your product are retained. These leads are then paired with the contact information of the buyers and pushed to the Compile dashboard, e-mail digest, or your CRM tool.

Other tools to check out in this category include **Mintigo** and **Mighty Signals**.

Use Your Network

There are a few solid products whose core business models are to provide you with full use of your professional networks.

This means you can use your friends and colleagues to facilitate warm introductions, effectively speeding up deal cycles.

Conspire

By connecting your e-mail account and allowing it to analyze your e-mail data, Conspire understands who you know, and how well. With that understanding, Conspire finds the strongest path of connections in your extended network to the people and companies you are trying to reach.

Landing deals early on at a start-up is difficult because potential customers don't know the company from a hole in the wall. In these cases a warm introduction is key to getting attention and, potentially, a meeting. The rep uses Conspire to prioritize leads according to how strong of an introduction they can get from their professional network (including current or former colleagues, friends, classmates, etc.) When the rep has strong paths they are able to get a meaningful introduction from someone who knows both the rep and the target well. This means the relationship with the potential customer starts with a high degree of trust.

Conspire is using data and science to understand the strength of connection between you and your friend, and your friend and your target. This will tell you whether this friend of yours can make a good enough introduction for you. Now you can know the best possible path to a warm introduction.

According to Alex Devkar, CEO of Conspire,

The problem with other professional networks is that they do not accurately reflect a person's real relationships. First, the model of sending a connection request and accepting means all connections look the same—whether you met someone for 5 minutes or worked with them closely for 5 years. Second, you have to manually maintain their list of connections by adding new ones and removing fading connections, which in practice does not happen.

A similar sentiment comes from Mark Roberge, CRO of Hubspot, who would rather have his reps sell to people they know, instead of focusing on pre-determined territories.

If you think about territories, they grew out sales teams who knocked on doors. That's the whole point. Put your people where the doors are. For whatever reason, it is still around. Either way you should organize your sales team by the buyer persona.

Having a usable network is a huge advantage. Make sure it's well-leveraged by your team and organization.

Also check out **KiteDesk** to see which business connections you could leverage to gain access to your Accounts in Salesforce. Connection strength is scored for to tell you your best possible access point.

Take a look at **ProLeads** to get a view of your best path to contact a lead and insights into what to put in the email.

Getting Information on Your Individual Prospect

Discover.ly

Discoverly has taken the place of Rapportive in my Gmail. It sits in Gmail as a browser extension and produces information from social accounts linked to the recipient's e-mail address.

Reps can also use this to quickly verify e-mails within Gmail by typing in the best-guessed e-mail address and seeing if a profile comes up.

Rapportive is still a valid option, but they haven't done much to keep their spot since the LinkedIn acquisition.

FullContact pulls from the social profiles of all of your contacts so you have all necessary social media information handy in your CRM. It's also great for syncing, cleaning, verifying, and de-duplicating contact lists.

For more on Trigger Events, and when and why to reach out, I recommend reading top posts from Craig Elias, Jamie Shanks, Jeff Hoffman, John Barrows, and Daniel Barber.

Chapter 6: Segmenting

The first message you send to the prospect is absolutely crucial. This first-touch e-mail really needs to work in your favor. The only way to personalize your messaging in a scalable manner is to get really good at segmenting your lists. This allows you to hit a full list with a note that is tailored to all of them, yet is still fairly general.

Here's an example of how a company called The Storefront used segmenting to properly personalize their message at scale.

The Storefront is a marketplace for pop-up shops and short-term retail rentals. When opening in new cities across the US, The Storefront needed to market their service to both landlords and retailers so they found websites where the contact details for landlords are listed (**Yelp**, **Tripadvisor**), and websites where the contact details for retailers are listed (**Etsy**, **Kickstarter**).

They then used Import.io to extract all contact details from the websites into neatly ordered lists, which they could export into Google Docs. When extracting contact details they also extract as much additional information about the lead as possible. They used this additional information to further segment lists so that they could create message templates that generated highly personalized messages for each lead.

One way they segmented the lists was by neighborhood. When building the list for New York City retail spaces, they scraped space listings from Yelp. This gave them all the contact information they needed and also grouped the leads by neighborhood. By pulling this information, they could put together a personalized template geared towards companies in specific areas of New York City, like Soho or Tribeca.

They would send an e-mail to the companies with a mention of the neighborhood they were in and the other stores in that neighborhood already listing on The Storefront. This made the message feel a lot more personal to the storeowner, but was still a mass message sent through an e-mail campaign.

For example, they could write, "We've been running pop-up shops with storeowners in [neighborhood] successfully for over two years now. Your neighbors [Store1] and [Store2] are also utilizing the marketplace to rent out their spaces."

The message seems personalized, but all of the information is pulled from the .csv you created. Nothing has to be manually filled in. This is the power of careful segmenting.

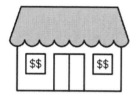  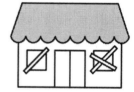

Where to Start Segmenting

Now that you have lists, contact information, and some research you should have a good idea of how to segment your lists. First separate out all the leads for which you have warm introductions. Using the tools from previous chapters you should be able to figure out to which accounts you can get introduced. That's probably your best way in, if you can get it.

Next, you can take a look at where you pulled the lists. For example, if you scraped the list of companies that sponsored at Dreamforce it is already a well-segmented list. You can use the fact that they sponsored in your message. In an e-mail to this full list you can say something like, "Companies that sponsor Dreamforce see X value with our product" or "I really enjoyed chatting with the reps in your booth at Dreamforce and I would love to continue the conversation." The context gives it some personalization. This requires that you segment the list properly.

Again, the deeper you can segment, the more personal you can get while still contacting multiple companies. If I took the Dreamforce list, then pulled out the companies on the list that perform a certain service I have a list that's even more targeted. Hence, my messaging could drill in on the fact that they were at Dreamforce and also perform a certain service, making the message look more personalized than before, while still hitting numerous companies.

Start playing with other reasons to segment lists at your company based on alerts, triggers, or how you built the lists in the first place.

I recently met with an e-commerce company out of Singapore called **TradeGecko**. They were getting plenty of inbound from e-cigarette companies wanting to use their backend Inventory Management Software. Using this information, they built a list of e-cigarette distributors in the US and UK for their first outbound sales campaign. This was a well-defined list with a targeted message, and it should have high success rates for them. They segmented on Location and Industry, but you can play around with it.

Since this was their first campaign, they did not have results to compare it to, however, they were blown away by the response. They had over 50% of the e-cigarette companies they reached sign up for a free trial of TradeGecko.

Deeper segmentation allows you to be more targeted with your messaging, leading to less spam complaints and higher positive response rates. It is extremely important to make sure you're sending e-mails that will elicit a positive response. Doing this at scale is a science and an art that can be mastered.

With new changes to their InMail policy, even LinkedIn is finally rewarding people for doing this the right way.

LinkedIn has said,

> *InMail credits will be returned for every response, rather than for no response: InMail messages that get any response (Reply or Not Interested) from a recipient within 90 days will be credited back to you. If you don't get a response within 90 days, however, the InMail credit will not be replaced.*

There aren't very many tools I've found to strictly help with segmenting lists. It's a very intuitive process that is up to you to decipher. It isn't hard, but the more you can think through the possibilities, and further segment your lists, the easier it will be to personalize messages at scale.

But What About Whales?

Here's the last point about segmenting lists for those with an average of large-sized deals or big partnerships.

Take the top accounts, maybe the top 10% or 100 accounts that you want to access and have really good information on, and e-mail them with really good, targeted e-mails. Save the mass e-mailing for the rest. For these big deals, you want to be spot-on and authentic. Provide value and really get them attracted from the get-go.

Sometimes, if you're lucky, your Low-hanging Fruit and Whales will overlap. I was working with a company looking to go after Corporate Learning and Development budget. The companies in this space are types like General Electric, Levis, and Coca-Cola, which each spend millions per year on internal training. All I had to do was visit competitors' websites that listed case-studies and quotes. Not only do we know the company has budget and is allocating it in this way, but by observing who the quotes came from, we also get the exact buyer's name and title at that company.

These leads would be in what I consider the top 10%.

Visit HackingSales.com/Resources for more information on finding contact info, conducting lead research, and segmenting your lists.

Chapter 7: Outbound E-mailing/Messaging

Ready? This is a long but incredibly important chapter.

To recap:

- You have your list of target companies
- You cleaned them for duplicates
- You know who at that company you want to reach
- You have their contact information
- You did your research
- You have the lists properly segmented

Now you'll learn:

- What types of messaging are effective in getting positive responses
- A/B testing and e-mail optimization
- What metrics to measure and how to use that information to take action
- Setting up a cadence and how often/long you can send e-mails
- The top tools in this space and how to use them
- How to turn negative responses into positive ones

You're ready to start activating your prospects, but before you send anything, you need to focus on your message. There are a lot of resources available that show you how to write cold e-mails.

For subject lines, check out these fun and insightful articles from Copyblogger, Hubspot, Buffer, and QuickSprout.

For the body of the e-mail, I recommend checking out the Boron Letters and Neville Medhora for AIDA copywriting help. See Heather R. Morgan and Bryan Kreuzberger for help on cold e-mail writing.

I'll provide more suggested reading in the resources section at the end of this book. For now, I won't go into example e-mails, as you can find those all over the Internet. I am going to focus on the topic of outbound e-mailing as a whole.

The tools used for Sales Automation have changed the game for those who embrace science in sales. You can track, measure, and optimize like never before. I can see when, where, and how long someone is reading my e-mail. If you have a link or a presentation, that can also be tracked. The level of visibility you can get these days is incredible. However, what really matters is what you decide to do with this information.

A/B testing and Optimizing E-mails

Before creating your campaign, it's best to understand the process. You'll want to test a few things:

- Opened or Viewed Rate—this is the strength of your subject line
- Click Through Rate—this is the strength of your call-to-action
- Response Rate—this is the strength of your message
    - For response rates, I usually only count positive or lukewarm responses. Negative responses like "take me off your list" don't count, but should be read for feedback purposes

The best way to optimize for each of these is to A/B or multi-variable test your e-mails and send them through one of the e-mail campaign tools so you can get accurate metrics. The previous segmenting we did was also helpful for these reasons:

- Segmenting, and results based on segmenting, helps you measure and optimize campaigns. Sometimes you'll just have a low performing segment or list for one reason or another.
- It's easier to send batches of e-mails. I recommend 50 to 100 per day, per single e-mail address. Less than 50 and your sample size is too small and you're going too slowly. More than 100 and you start to trigger spam filters in Gmail.

The first thing to start with is the subject line. Take a subset of your lists, at least 50 to 100 e-mails per test, and start sending the same e-mail, but with different subject lines. Do this 4 times. Then take the one with the highest open rate and use that one as the baseline in a new test with 3 other subject lines.

I like to use the Appropriate Person or Introduction Request subject lines from earlier in the book as my baseline to test against. These subject lines have been shared all over the Internet so I'm surprised they still work, but they do. The goal is to get open rates at a minimum of 30%.

Keep testing until you get there, but don't stoop to low levels just to get high open rates. Using an artificial forward or reply is a way to dupe someone, and they know that. If you play tricks, you'll abuse their trust before you ever get a chance to open dialogue, and that's not going to bode well for you.

One thing to test is using the person's name or the company name in the subject lines. This makes the e-mail look more personal before they even open it.

Next, test different locations and languages for your call-to-action, using either links or attachments. Try to make sure your e-mails look like casual e-mails and not marketing e-mails when you do this.

Lastly, the body of the message should be short and to the point. Don't give too much information. Provide value for them, feel their pain, talk about them—not to yourself. If you did your research and you are reaching out individually instead of mass-e-mailing, then you should know what their initial problems might be.

Always go into this opening e-mail with the goal of setting up the first call. Do not aim too high or ask for too much. Be strong and lay out a certain time to speak. Don't ask.

Even though you are collecting information on Open, Click-through, and Response Rates the only thing that you need to worry about in your pipeline is number of meetings that you set up. You are using all of these e-mail metrics to make your e-mails better so that you set up more meetings.

The numbers will vary by who you ask and the type of business, but you'll want to aim for numbers like these:

- Open Rate: 30 to -50% of 100%
- Click Through Rate: 20 to 35% of 100%

- Response Rate: 15 to 30% of 100%
- Meetings Setup Rate: 10 to 20% of 100%

There are many other variables at play here that could lead to skewed numbers. Some of the variables are:

- Poor performing lists
- Server or sending issues
- Rep sending the e-mails
- Time of day/date

To counteract some of these variables, do research. According to the sales automation company, Yesware, your e-mail has a very low chance of being opened if it hasn't been read within the first 24 hours.

Many advise sending e-mails at 9:00 a.m. local time on Tuesday and Wednesday. Some like to send e-mails around 3:00 to 6:00 p.m. local time on Tuesday and Wednesday to catch people as they're getting out of work. Others say that sending e-mails on weekends is best, since people don't get a lot of e-mail then and that yours will stand out more.

There are many different studies and justifications for e-mail campaign timing. I recommend you take advice from a few sources and see what works best for your audience. Again, you can always lean on your allies. Don't be afraid to ask what works for people in the space that aren't competitors. Save yourself some time.

```
I WILL TEST, MEASURE, AND OPTIMIZE
I WILL TEST, MEASURE, AND OPTIMIZE
I WILL TEST, MEASURE, AND OPTIMIZE
I WILL TEST, MEASURE, AND OPTIMIZE
I WILL TEST, MEASURE, AND...
```

Determining Your Perfect Cadence

These outbound sales campaigns also go by cadences or sequences and are run through e-mail automation software. I'll go over the tools in the space soon, but first here's some high-level strategy to understand.

When setting up y outbound sales campaigns you'll need to pick a number of touches per lead and decide how to contact them.

Recently, Hubspot ran a study that said after nine touches you've reached the point of diminishing returns. In the advertising world they say the customer needs to see your brand seven times before they can start to recognize it.

Tawheed Kader, the CEO at ToutApp, calls his cadence the five by five. Kyle Porter, the CEO of SalesLoft, calls his cadence the seven by seven.

According to Kevin Gaither, VP of Inside Sales at ZipRecruiter,

Most outbound reps give up after one to three attempts to a lead, but statistics from InsideSales.com and Velocify show that you'll need six to nine touches to establish contact and qualify the lead. Once you've made your six to nine touches over a three-week period, only then should you put your lead into a Nurture Queue for follow up at a later date.

John Barrows, one of the leading sales trainers and SDR trainers for Salesforce, Marketo, LinkedIn, Box, Zendesk, and more says to keep contacting them until they give you a response or a definitive "no." Then he'll still follow up again in a few months.

I tend to agree with John here, I think the best salespeople are persistent to a tee. In sales, "no" is the second best answer. "Yes" is the first, but a "maybe" or not receiving an answer are by far the worst.

This seems to be something nobody in sales can agree on, but I think it's something that should be different for every business. It depends on deal size, pipeline, number of leads/active leads, and other factors. This is where you can play around and see what's best for you.

Now here's where segmenting comes into play again. You'll have maybe two to three groupings of leads. The top group, your whales or low-hanging fruit F500 companies, like in the segmenting example, would get phone calls built into their campaign. The next grouping down would strictly get e-mails, but with a high personal touch (meaning, deeply segmented, or somewhat customized). The bottom group would go into a standard outbound drip campaign from the rep until they respond.

I don't like calling everyone, but some do. I think you really need to have extra resources for that to work well. If you're an individual rep with a territory at a big company, go ahead and call everyone. But if you're a co-founder or early stage sales hire, you're probably spread too thin to call every single outbound lead.

I also don't like stopping a cadence, but some do. Only when they reply do people get taken off the list. If it's a hard "no," you can reach back out in six to nine months to see if the timing is better. As the campaign goes on, time between e-mails should lengthen to a maximum of two weeks. Basically, if you're hitting the right person with the right message at the right time you shouldn't stop until you have the hardest "no." The Industry has very different opinions, but it depends on your company, process, sell, and personnel. I like to call the biggest leads first, then send the smaller leads e-mails until we set up a warm call.

The Services That Power Outbound Sales

This is one of my favorite categories of tools because of how useful they all are. Each one of these companies has the potential to be a billion-dollar company and best friend of salespeople everywhere.

Users can build and optimize e-mail templates, A/B test, track, and send e-mails to groups of prospects at once. Some of them have much deeper analytics for managers, which we won't get into much. Many integrate with Salesforce, Gmail, Outlook, and other CRMs, so they should be able to handle whatever systems your company is built on.

Enterprise/Cross Organization

These tools are being use across organizations, not just in sales.

ToutApp

Over the last three years, ToutApp has been able to develop a pretty robust and invaluable sales tool that is now being used across entire organizations. They built an incredible team out of San Francisco that has done an amazing job at growing sales reps who had little previous experience. Without much funding and only one full-time developer, they've come a long, long way.

Some of the more advanced features are:

- A Live Feed, so users can see in real-time when someone opened their e-mail, clicked on a link, opened the attachment, what page of the attachment they read, and what page of their website is being viewed.
- Group e-mails that can easily be searched for all those who haven't responded, so a follow-up message can be sent to them.
- Visual tracking of prospects' engagement through their views, clicks, and replies.
- Niko scrapes contact information from any website and ensures that Tout and Salesforce are always up to date.

Tout plugs directly into both Gmail and Outlook and has a deep integration with Salesforce, so that reps and managers can access Tout data and tools from anywhere they like. ToutApp also integrates with marketing automation platforms like Marketo, so that Sales and Marketing can stay in sync and see what messaging is resonating best with prospects to move them through the funnel.

Featured Use Cases:

Using tracking with Tout, a director of hospitality sales at an NBA franchise was able to close two six-figure deals in one month, which he wouldn't have been able to close otherwise. With the first, he was able to see his e-mail being forwarded to multiple people at the prospect, and that they were actively engaged and interested, so he gave them time to continue gathering information, and then followed up at the right time.

With another prospect, he was having a hard time getting in touch with someone that he already knew would be interested in purchasing a suite. The prospect went dark with no contact for several months until he popped up on his Live Feed one day. The director called him while he was looking at his e-mail and closed the deal on the same call.

Yesware

Yesware is another one of the big boys in the space that has only been around for a few short years but has created a great product for the modern salesperson. They have double the headcount of ToutApp and have raised four times as much money. They are based in Boston and now have offices in San Francisco as well.

Some of the more advanced features are:

- Yesware Mobile allows sales reps to send and track e-mails and access the templates through their mobile device. Activity is automatically synced with Salesforce data.
- Swipe-to-call allows a rep to call a prospect directly from an e-mail thread. Yesware's data shows responding to a recently opened e-mail results in a 30% higher connection rate. This tool allows a salesperson to quickly reach out once an e-mail event takes place, even while on the go.
- Yesware's presentation tracking feature gives deep insight into how engaged a prospect is with any content shared. Sales teams are able to see how many people were sent the presentation, how many views the presentation received, and the average time spent viewing the presentation.

Significant use yields larger amounts of data collected, which builds a more complete picture for reps and managers analyzing individual performance, team performance, best practices, progress over time, etc.

In addition, Yesware provides actionable insights. For example, Yesware's data shows that Monday isn't the best day to send an e-mail—the highest number of e-mail opens are on the weekends.

Featured Use Case:

Acquia took advantage of the e-mail-tracking feature to collect data around various events, like e-mail opens, link clicks, and attachment views. This granular information allowed Acquia to take a great deal of the guesswork out of the sales process, resulting in fewer touches to move a deal through the pipeline.

That information also made it easier for sales reps to prioritize prospects and determine next steps, including when they should call.

Reps that called a prospect immediately after the prospect opened an e-mail, clicked a link, or opened an attachment connected with that prospect over 34% of the time. Overall, Acquia's use of Yesware data to determine who and when to call improved reps' overall call connection rate by 29%.

Sidekick **(from Hubspot)**

Hubspot's Sidekick is a little different than the other Enterprise players. Their claim to fame is that their product is made more for the rep, not for the manager.

Brian Balfour who leads Growth for Sidekick explains,
> *Sales reps need tools that make their day faster, more productive, and more efficient. We developed a tool with the sales rep in mind, growing adoption through the frontline sellers, and learning what their specific needs are.*

Sidekick has an activity feed for reps to get notified about actions in real-time. Obviously they have deep integrations in Hubspot's Marketing and CRM software as well as Salesforce. If you're already heavily reliant on Hubspot, this might be a good option for you.

A unique integration that I really like is its connection with Zapier, Sidekick syncs with the various tools and apps available through the Zapier app exchange. For example, sales reps can sync Twitter and Sidekick to get custom Tweet notifications in their Activity Stream, and it also syncs with Zendesk to get support case information.

Sales and Customer Success

These tools were built for the Sales organization, more specifically the SDR teams:

Outreach.io

Outreach.io is a really strong new player in the space with a solid team and sturdy product. The key difference is that instead of firing a pixel, like all other e-mail tracking software companies, they hook into your SMTP server. RelateIQ did this in the CRM space. They've found that this gives you better and more accurate data on your replied rates. It's also fairly intuitive. It filters out duplicate e-mails automatically and gives you recommendations on the best times to send your e-mails, and how many to send.

Featured Use Case:

The sales team at Datanyze was looking to automate cold outbound outreach and put it on cruise control. They wanted to create a series of touch-points that would stop upon reply from the prospect.

They had two requirements:

- Reply detection had to be bulletproof. They could not afford an e-mail going out to a prospect who had already engaged with sales.
- They needed to be able to easily A/B test their e-mails and change things on the fly. Their team is extremely metrics-driven and wanted to use testing as a way to improve conversion from current leads.

Since using Outreach for outbound sales, Datanyze has hit 50% reply rates for cold e-mails—a number that had previously been impossible to achieve.

Outreach also serves as the mid-funnel sales touchpoint for inbound teams. SDR/MDR teams have the ability to reply to inbound leads with one to one personalized sales e-mails coming directly from the sales rep based on lead attributes.

It integrates with Salesforce, Outlook, and Gmail.

Cadence **(from SalesLoft)**

I went over SalesLoft's Prospecting and Lead Gen tool in Chapter 4, but recently they've released a new product that allows you to take those leads and start prospecting. Their tool is built directly for both the SDR on outbound and inbound, and helps them not only with e-mail contact, but with voice as well.

For example, you can set up and run a campaign inside of Cadence that consists of e-mails and calls that looks like this:

- Day 1: E-mail
- Day 2: Call in the morning
- Day 3: Call in the morning without voicemail; call in the afternoon with voicemail.
- Etc.

Featured Use Case:

Insightpool has dedicated their entire outbound sales process to the Cadence tool. It's the application of record for their SDR team helping them create, maintain, and improve on their call and e-mail process. The system gives the reps a simple process to follow for e-mail templates, tracking and analytics, power phone call dialing with voice recording, notes storage, and sync with CRM.

Check out SalesLoft's Top Secret SDR Playbook for guidance on setting up your Cadence.

PersistIQ

PersistIQ is another interesting up-and-comer in the SDR space. The product is well built with key features like de-duplicating e-mails and showing your previous conversations with that lead from Salesforce. The product is very similar to Outreach and Cadence.

CEO Pouyan Selehi says they built PersistIQ because,
> We think reps should focus on the quality of your outbound sales instead of just quantity. This means take the time to think through and create prospect profiles and create targeted messages. Try different messages, wait different periods of time between touchpoints, and segment differently. Find what works for you.

Sendbloom

Sendbloom is the outlier in this SDR space. Their goal is to allow you to deeper segment your lists and engage with the prospects at scale. Their system actually builds in more data about your leads for you, and then helps you figure out how to segment your lists and craft messaging that will create action in that specific segment.

Sendbloom helps sales and market development teams nurture target accounts and stay on top of inbound leads. SDR teams need to know that there is no one-size-fits-all message. With Sendbloom, these SDRs can create conditional segments for their leads based on criteria like the prospect's title and analytics stack. The product is doing this research for them programmatically and only the prospects that don't reply receive another message.

Also check out **Selligy**.

For syncing e-mails directly to Salesforce and vice versa check out **Cirrus Insight**, **Groove**.

For testing how e-mails will look on different devices, e-mail clients, and browsers checkout **E-mail on Acid** and **Litmus**.

Quick Tips on Messaging Psychology

1. Pay very close attention to the words you use.

Think about this for a second. If we're partnering on a project, and I tell you you're going to have a lot of responsibility you'll see that as daunting and high-pressure. If I tell you you'll have a lot of control, you see that as freeing and might be enthusiastic. It means the same thing, it just comes off differently to the other person.

2. Keep it short and dumb it down.

Nobody wants to hear your jargon and abbreviation riddled, multi-paragraph sales pitch. Even worse is when salespeople start using big words to sound smarter or more knowledgeable. In the end you lose people. You're not making it easy enough on them.

Keep things easily readable for your recipient so they can digest the information quickly and take action. Imagine that your recipient is reading it on their smart phone on the bus ride home after a long day at the office. You'll want to make sure your message is short and easy to read. That's the only way that they'll read it through and take action.

Be sure to make the key points and preferred actions clear, **maybe even highlight them in bold**.

Thinking about using the word "utilize"? The word "use" is fine.

Don't use abbreviations unless they're universally well known in the industry, like CRM or ROI. Things like CLTV, CACR, ACAC are not as well known, so stay away from anything the recipient might not understand.

Don't be afraid to go against the principles of writing in your e-mails. This isn't your high school honors English class; this is an important message to a busy potential buyer. Try adding more spacing in your e-mails—separate paragraphs every two sentences. Make it easy for them to scan or read quickly.

Make the message simple enough for an eight year old to understand.

3. Don't be afraid to challenge people.

When setting up an outbound campaign or setting up to do sales in general, you'll need to have a thick skin and sometimes a short memory. There will always be people who reply with a poor attitude. Just keep pushing, and do it the right way. You're just doing your job, and know that for every one person that responds negatively, you'll sign up 50 more.

Don't ignore those people, either. Sometimes a great way to reply is by challenging them.

At Udemy, we would get poor replies from experts all the time. As we refined our process there were fewer and fewer negative replies, but it still happened once in a while. If you could read the situation well, and knew a little bit about their background, sometimes you could flip them. One thing I used to respond with was a challenge. I would find two big-name experts in their space that they knew, and reply as such:

Hi [First name],

Sorry to have bothered you. I thought you were on the level of [expert 1] and [expert 2] who are both doing extremely well on Udemy. That's why I thought this would be perfect for you, but I guess I was mistaken.

I will make sure you do not receive another e-mail from us.

Again, I apologize.

Best,
Max

In this case, you're challenging them by saying if they do not see the value, they must not be such a big expert. Some people will call your bluff and not respond, and others will respond with a simple "thanks." But sometimes, and more often than not, you'll get the response, "Oh I didn't know [expert 1] and [expert 2] were on Udemy. Maybe I have a few minutes to chat this week."

4. Sell to the Individual, then the Employee, then the Company.

The person on the other end of your message is an individual first and foremost. He or she is a human being with feelings, emotions, wants, and needs. Appeal to the individual first, making them feel like they'll be more special or important if they listen to you. Then appeal to their career side, and how it will make them look good to their boss. Lastly, appeal to the company side by providing them with the tools they need to sell the rest of the company on your product.

For example, Here's how this is going to make you look like a hero to your team. Here's how it's going to make your team more productive and generate more revenue. Here's how to sell it to the key stakeholders.

Here are a few more things to note when conveying a message via e-mail, from cold e-mail expert and CEO of Salesfolk, Heather R. Morgan:

- *Make your e-mail conversational and human. Don't write like a robot or be gimmicky like a marketer.*
- *Be persuasive. Try to evoke emotions.*
- *Talk about your product or service in terms of benefits instead of features. For example: "use this process to triple your response rates" vs "this feature helps with AB testing to write better e-mail copy"*
- *It's more convincing to show your benefits in the form of a case study sentence, instead of telling them. Use a*

stat if possible. For example: "Our e-mail copy helped [Client] double their qualified leads in a month, which also doubled their sales team's quota."

- *Try to add value, evoke fear of loss, or play on people's competitive nature.*
- *Be focused and don't try to cover too many tangential points in one e-mail.*
- *Develop a clear persona for each segment list.*
- *One concept/idea per e-mail. If you have a lot of value props and ideas; relax, just save them for other touches in your campaign.*
- *Send six to eight e-mails for every person you're reaching out to.*
- *In some cases, you might actually get more responses in e-mails six to eight than any other touch point earlier in your campaign. Even if this isn't the case, it's still worth it to get the people who respond on e-mail six to eight that would have otherwise stayed cold.*
- *Test everything. Every persona and industry is different, so you need to test things to find out what works.*
- *Stay away from long sentences or long paragraphs.*
- *Don't be afraid to ask for things or demand things, just do it politely.*
  - *The difference between pushy and persistence is politeness.*
- *Try putting the company name in the subject line.*

Visit HackingSales.com/Resources for more on cold outreach and outbound email campaign guidance.

Chapter 8: Sales Outsourcing

If you look back through the past few chapters, you'll start to pick out tasks all over the place that are menial and tedious. This is a where a virtual assistant (VA) comes in and every organization, no matter how small, should be leveraging these cheap but qualified workers.

At Udemy, we employed a lead generation team of 12 virtual SDRs. They did everything from lead generate to actually send batches of e-mails and set up meetings. Eventually they spread across the entire company, doing everything from website bug testing to instructor support.

I have a team of three to four VAs working at all times. They're such an asset and can do anything in the sales process. If you can nail this piece of the process it's to your major unfair advantage as a salesperson or sales organization.

Here are a few tasks they can do right off the bat:
1. Use Import.io or Kimono Labs, they just need links to lists
2. Get leads from any of the lead generation tools using the lists they've built
3. Do lead research by uploading lists into any of the tools in the lead research section
4. Segment and de-duplicate lists based on your orders
5. Upload lists into sales automation software, and even set up sequences

Yup, they can do almost the entire SDR process up until the actual call. You need to come up with the ICP and where they live, give the VAs the links, tell the VAs how to segment the lists, then craft the content.

That's it. And they work for between $3.50 and $7 per hour. Yup. It's that cheap. Don't feel bad, either. That's a great salary in the Philippines, where I exclusively hire my VAs.

Preparing to Hire Virtual Assistants

First thing you'll want to do when getting ready to hire a VA is to draw out the current process for everything you'd like to hand off. Once you draw out these tasks on paper, you'll also be able to see what you can cut, if anything. This is Pareto's law at work, most of what you do for your business is busy work. 20% of your work leads to 80% of your results, whether that is in customers or revenue.

Find out what your bread and butter is—your 20%—and either cut or delegate the rest. If you can't get organized and draw this out for yourself then you're probably doing something wrong to begin with.

Hiring Virtual Assistants

You can hire VAs for all sorts of things. I'm going to break down the right ways to hire VAs and the right areas to hire them from (both web services and longitude/latitude).

oDesk

oDesk has a fully-stocked marketplace of great talent. You can find some of the best VAs there at a bargain.

The backend is pretty robust as well. They boast the best time-tracking and payment-tracking tools of any of the outsourcing sites. This makes it best for managing overseas employees that are working alongside you. I've had my VA's logging 40 to 60 hours of work per week and usually working during our hours. It's very easy to build out a full team on oDesk. You set the price in the beginning and that's what you end up paying per hour.

Suggested Projects:
- Lead Generation/Link Building
- Customer Support
- QA Testing Engineer

My advice is to hire only from the Philippines. VAs from the Philippines are primarily good for outsourcing tasks like lead building, especially if they are using Google Apps or Microsoft Office. Most of them are great at Excel and even had previous careers as nurses or professionals. At $3 an hour you can get some solid work done, just make things super clear. At $5 an hour, you can get VAs as competent as most U.S. college students, no exaggeration. That extra two bucks could be worth it for your business. I pay my manager $7 an hour and she's all-pro.

TaskUs

We started using TaskUs at Udemy early on and found that they employ extremely high quality virtual assistants that can do tasks all around the organization. TaskUs gives you a fully managed backend and helps you hire out the team. All you have to do is train and manage. This is a pretty good scenario if you don't want to deal with any logistical headaches like finding talent and paying through the Philippines. Services like oDesk do take a big fee (11%). So for getting good talent and not having to deal with the backend logistics, TaskUs might be worth it for you.

They work with big tech companies such as Udemy, Eventbrite, and Adroll.

Suggested Projects: Everything, but they're a little pricier. You're looking at about $10 an hour. They're good, though.

LeadGenius

LeadGenius couples proprietary data and technology with a dedicated team of outsourced sales reps. They work with your sales development team to feed higher-quality leads into a company's existing sales funnel, no matter how you have it structured. Their core offering is higher-quality customer data.

Outside of the outsourced SDR, they help existing teams prioritize MQLs, identify buying signals for previously untapped audiences, or segment existing marketing lists for more intelligent targeting. They can also manage e-mail outreach for clients who do not have that element built into their sales funnel.

CEO of LeadGenius, Anand Kulkarni, adds, "There is always room for increased efficiency at the top of the funnel, be it in researching companies, data gathering, lead quality, or handling initial outreach."

Featured Use Case:

LeadGenius supplied Signifyd with their own dedicated on-demand prospecting team to deliver hundreds of carefully chosen leads each week. Signifyd worked with their dedicated LeadGenius team to identify the most likely to convert segments of their buying audience. Instead of turning on a firehose of contacts, LeadGenius provided the Signifyd sales team with a prioritized list of prospects that were converting at double or triple the rate.

After working with LeadGenius for only five months, Signifyd saw these results:

- 2690 leads were sourced, saving their team 851 hours of research
- 2436 of those leads were contacted (91%)
- 148 of those leads resulted in sales demos (6%)

GoodCall.io

GoodCall.io is a turnkey solution for your entire SDR sales process. They pair you with a team of virtual assistants they call Lucy that leverage a pre-built and vetted database of leads, proven and tested e-mail templates, automated follow-ups, and reporting to target accounts and get you qualified leads.

This allows in-house reps to spend less time doing menial, trigger follow-up type tasks and more actual selling.

Carb.io

Carb.io, also known as Carburetor, is the new kid on the block and is modelled after Aaron Ross's book, *Predictable Revenue*. He's actually a co-founder and partner of the product.

They help you fill the top of the funnel by figuring out your Ideal Customer Profile and then set out to find those leads and other low-hanging fruit across the web. They have an internal sales team that reaches out on your behalf and activates the prospect. Once the prospect replies, they introduce you.

Think of it as Sales Development as a Service.

Fiverr

On Fiverr.com, yes that's two "r's," you can hire people to do all sorts of weird and unique things for you for just five bucks. If you want them to do it quicker, or more of it, they charge in $5 increments.

You can use Fiverr to find someone that will do small projects or build small e-mail lists for $5 per task.

You can choose who to hire based on reviews and whether they can do your project. Physical location doesn't matter as much on Fiverr. Don't bother bargaining, it's five bucks!

If you have a long process like an entire sales pipeline, you might want to try breaking it up and hiring multiple virtual assistants for it. I've found it's best to hire for the exact thing that they are doing instead of making them learn a ton of different things. You can test this if you wish.

You can pay more and have someone do the whole process, or pay less per VA and have a few do parts of the process. You can also limit their hours so you don't get charged like crazy. However, with more VAs comes more management. Play around a bit and figure out what works best for your process. My advice is to hire one rockstar to begin with and train them on the whole process. Get them really good at it. Then they can go off and train and manage new VAs.

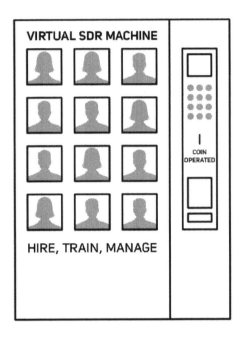

Here's a sample job posting for a lead generation task that I put on oDesk.

Title: Full-time Filipino Lead Generator/Researcher
Job Description:

About Us:
Our company xxxxxxxxxxxxx

Where You Fit In:
We are looking for someone to help generate leads for xxxxxxxxxx

- Should be proficient in Excel and comfortable working in Google Docs
- Must have solid Internet connection 24/7—we mainly communicate via Skype and e-mail and expect you to be online and available during the day
- Must be able to communicate in English
- Past researching or lead generation experience is a huge plus
- Must be able to work Monday through Friday, 9:00 am to 5:00 pm Pacific Standard Time, as we are based in San Francisco.
- Please send me a link to past work.

We work with a few other tools/sites:
- Rapportive in Gmail
- Google Docs
- Salesforce
- Web scrapers and Import.io
- Twitter
- ToutApp

You should be able to pick these up quickly or already have prior experience with them.

Task Example:
We might ask you to find people with Twitter followings or Facebook fan pages of over 20K likes/followers. We will want them in personal finance, personal development, business, or technology verticals.

Your job will be to find these people and create a lead list with their names, community size, type of vertical, link to their company, and e-mail address. We will also have you check our database for duplicates.

Pay:
We will offer between $3 to $5 per hour depending on experience and candidate selection.

If this seems like something you will be amazing at, please apply to this job post, take this brief test, and fill out the test form below.

Test:
Find the names, number of Twitter followers, and e-mail addresses for 10 people on this list:
www.link.com/peoplethatareawesome

Test Form:
https://docs.google.com/forms/d/1sSPA-r9VbxYYEc5U6P_RGjpaBa5RM5s6482BW9-GwnE/viewform
Thanks and we look forward to working with you!
Super Fun Udemy Family

Skills Required:
English, Microsoft Excel, lead-generation, Internet-research, data-scraping, keyword-research, data-mining, salesforce.com, google-docs

Notes on this Job Posting

- Workers from the Philippines are best for this type of task. Most have moved on from legitimate jobs like nursing and almost all have been to college.

- Some people like to give an exact direction in the description to test if the applicant even read the posting, for example your description would say, "When replying to the post, please send a cover letter and make the first line read, I'm a rock star lead-machine and I am ready to rock!" This is supposed to show the employer that they read the post and pay attention to detail.
- Most will work during your hours.
- I start them at 40 hours but usually increase to 60 hours per week when they've earned my trust.
- I like to insert a form into the job description. It's easy to do and timestamps their response. Make sure your first questions is "Name as it appears on oDesk" so you know who responded. I use Google Forms.
- Mention the software you use so they know what to expect.

After about 12 hours you'll have between 25 to 50 candidates. I usually pick the top few and ask them to Skype with me before I hire them. This is when I can give them a timed task, which is the most important part. We know how many leads per hour is strong for us, so a 20-minute sprint test is a good way to see if they can keep pace.

Training your Virtual Assistants

When training your VAs, you must give them exact directions and set goals that are easy to track. This is the only way to make sure you've selected a good VA. If you hire more than one, you'll start to have a sample size and will know what to expect.

The best way to start is to do the task yourself and see how long it takes. If you're having the VAs do lead generation, you can set up the process and pipeline, and do the task yourself for an hour or until you hit a certain number of leads. Time yourself or count how many leads you've generated in the hour and that's how many leads you should expect from a good VA.

For example, if it takes you an hour to collect 100 leads, then you know have a frame of reference. If it takes your VA two hours to collect 100 leads, then they're probably not very good. It's not unrealistic for them to be as good or even better than you at this task, especially if they've done this before.

This will also allow you to create really solid directions to document the process and take screenshots or screencasts with Jing or Skitch as you go. I like to create a step-by-step training manual that has everything they need to know, as granular as possible. This should also have all of the logins and passwords that they'll need to know.

If the test and the manual are good enough and they've been doing a similar job in the past, you shouldn't need to train them much. I like to just give them the information and the task and let them get started. I encourage them to ask me questions in the beginning. The first few you train will help you refine the process to the point where future VAs won't have many questions or, if they do, one of the other VAs should know the answer. That's why I advise to get a rock star for the first VA.

If I have multiple VAs working for me at the same time, I can invite them to a group Skype chat or Google Group to answer their questions. This way I might not even have to answer because another VA will know the answer or, if I do have to answer, they will all now know how to resolve the issue.

Make sure to do one-on-one's with them from time to time. Matt Ellsworth, former VP of Growth at The Storefront, likes to do an exercise called Stop, Start, Continue with VAs. It goes, Stop doing X, Start Doing Y, Continue doing Z. This is a good way to give feedback to any employee, but especially works well with VAs.

Visit HackingSales.com/Resources for more help on hiring, training, and managing Virtual Assistants.

Chapter 9: Customer Relationship Management Software

The CRM space is crowded, and rightfully so. Jason Lemkin of SaaStr has stated that there can be multiple IPOs in this space, even for companies that fight for the bottom of the market. With one company, Salesforce, on track to do $10 Billion in ARR soon, I believe him.

Good CRMs can be debated all day long. At the start-up level, early stage to growth stage, you're pretty good with any of these alternatives. They're affordable, well-built, and boast an intuitive user experience.

PipelineDeals

PipelineDeals was designed to make your team more productive. The software is incredibly simple and easy to use, so you can get the most out of your data. It's also extremely flexible and customizable. If you have a somewhat unique sales process, odds are, it can support your style. It can do everything you would need a CRM to do.

It offers many integrations, which allow you to connect to the apps you already use or try something new. They integrate with Outlook and Google Apps, as well as e-mail marketing software, such as Mailchimp.

Their well-built mobile product for both iPhone and Android is easy to use for reps on the go.

Close.io

Close.io has a few core features as part of their CRM that differentiates them from other CRMs. They offer VoIP calling out of the box, two-way e-mail sync, and automatically log all calls and e-mails to avoid any manual data entry.

They've also built a search engine that enables everyone on the team to answer any questions on the fly. For example, Close.io can give you a result to the question, "Show me all leads with active opportunities that I've e-mailed longer than a week ago, haven't responded, and where the last call was at least seven days ago and 10 minutes long." That can be a pretty powerful feature when sorting through CRM data.

I recently learned that some customers actually use Close.io in conjunction with Salesforce, which enables them to get both the powerful backend of Salesforce and the user experience of Close.io.

Pipedrive

Pipedrive is known for the extreme pipeline visibility it gives the user. The sweet spot of Pipedrive is managing high-value deals and making sure balls don't get dropped at any stage of the sales cycle. This is achieved by getting a clear picture of the sales pipeline to identify opportunities and potential issues, as well as features that encourage planning follow-ups.

Udemy, was one of their first users. I was drawn to the way I could get a bird's-eye view of my entire pipeline. This is super helpful for small teams with big deals.

If you're using other web apps, you can use Zapier to connect all sorts of tools to Pipedrive and move your data automatically. For example, Pipedrive allows you to send MailChimp campaigns directly from the CRM using custom filters to easily create segments to send to.

BaseCRM

Base is a simple and easy to use CRM. It's a turnkey solution that offers a unique suite of tools for both the rep and manager.

Whether it's the initial prospecting, where reps clip leads from LinkedIn into Base, or complex sales analysis, Base can do it. It's also adaptable to all industries and sales processes from field sales to inside sales and more.

Jason Mills, Head of Sales at Expensify, says:

> *Base gives our team one central place to connect with prospects and customers, whether it's a call or an e-mail. Base also gives us a highly automated way to score and prioritize incoming prospects. Perhaps most importantly, the reporting in Base gives us immense insights into how our geographically-dispersed team operates, especially in terms of the areas for improvement.*

RelateIQ

In 2014, Salesforce acquired RelateIQ for a whopping $390 million, but the service is still going strong. RelateIQ integrates really well with other services you're using, without the need for an external integrations tool. The best integration is via your e-mail's SMTP server, similar to Outreach.io. This allows them to pull in information from your e-mail and calendar and give you a clear look at your data for each lead.

Their filtering and their Gmail extension are probably their strongest assets. It's nice when you can use a CRM from Gmail without having to open new tabs. The CRM filtering was built in an intuitive way that allows you to sift through data both accurately and easily.

Salesforce and Salesforce for Start-ups

Salesforce for Start-ups is coming out soon, so I'm excited to see what they have in store. I foresee most companies making the switch to Salesforce at some point, as it's super scalable. Plus, when you hire a VP of Sales, you usually let them pick their CRM of choice. Many of them come from companies that used Salesforce, so they already know it well. As one CEO once told me after he hired his first VP of Sales, "If you hire Roger Federer, you let him choose his racket."

Salesforce's downside is that it's not made for start-ups at the moment. The price is too high and the implementation is too difficult and time consuming to set up. It's a big investment all around.

The upside is endless scalability, both with data and hiring people who've worked in sales before. They can usually pick it up and get running full-speed immediately.

Streak is a simple CRM built directly into your inbox if you're looking for something move basic and easy to use.

Other CRMs that are good for large, rapidly scaling organizations include **Zoho** and **SugarCRM**.

Integration Software

This topic isn't big enough to get its own chapter, but if you know what you're doing, and can take advantage of integrations with your CRM, you can be 100 times more efficient in your sales process. These integrations let your tools talk to each other and trade information automatically.

Bedrock Data

Bedrock Data is great for your larger integrations that involve a ton of data. Unlocking this data-sharing potential between your CRM and other tools has huge potential. For example, you can use them to create a custom integration such as Hubspot to Salesforce to Recurly to Quickbooks, which is super powerful and will save your team tons of time in the long run.

Also, they've built a great team and product from some former Hubspot employees.

Zapier

Zapier, as mentioned earlier in the book, can also be used for integrations of all types—not only in your CRM, but in many stages of the sales process. You can use a simple one like notes from **Evernote** that sync to your CRM, or get a little crazier with any of these integrations:

- Form software (Wufoo, Typeform, Google Forms)
- Support services (Asana, Zendesk)

- Chat services (Slack, Hipchat)
- Marketing Automation (Mailchimp, Customer.io, Vero)
- And much more

Also check out IFTTT (IF This Than That) for smaller integrations like Evernote to Gmail. If you can master integration and web scraping solutions you'll have access to clean and actionable data across the entire the Internet. This is a huge unfair advantage over your peers.

Chapter 10: Nurturing Leads and Sparking Engagement

You're at the point now where you've finally started your outbound e-mail campaigns and are starting to see responses come back. Maybe your higher-level targets haven't responded yet, but some of your campaigns are working.

At this point you'll need to do a balance of prospecting into new leads, nurturing active accounts, and facilitating the deal for engaged potential buyers.

For prospecting into new leads, keep doing what you've been doing: Build lists, segment, and test and optimize e-mail campaigns.

For nurturing and facilitating the deal, we have a whole new job to do.

Using Social Media to Trigger Buyer Activity

Even if you haven't spoken to your lead yet, you'll want them to keep seeing your name and your company's name everywhere they go. First, make sure to surround them on social media accounts. Get out there and engage with them on LinkedIn and Twitter. Don't use Facebook, Instagram, or more personal sites because that will make you look too much like a stalker.

JOE SMITH
@Imabigdeal
CEO at BigCo. Buys a lot.
Makes big decisions.

Like, share, retweet, and favorite their content from time to time, allowing a few days between each post. You can even add this to your outbound campaign cadence and daily routine. This is a great task for a virtual assistant. If you use a sales automation tool with a live feed, you can have a VA do one or multiple social actions every time an action associated with that account appears on the live feed.

For example, if I see on the live feed that someone opened my e-mail, they should get a retweet and a like on their last LinkedIn comment right away. Maybe that will prompt them to take a deeper look at the e-mail or write back. You can also use the action you see in the live feed as a reason to call them immediately, but that goes without saying. This is more scalable, and allows you to nurture leads at scale.

You can use a tool such as Socedo, mentioned earlier in this book, to try doing this automatically.

Another thing you should be doing is sending them information, news, or content that is relevant to them. You can do this on a per-prospect basis, but that can be very time consuming. Only do this for your largest accounts. You should be able to find articles that are relevant to entire list segments that you can send out.

Find triggers or action events to use as a contact excuse. These triggers are the same as the ones mentioned earlier in this book. If the company raises money, expands, gets good PR, etc. then a congratulations from you is in order. Make sure to take advantage of these trigger events, as they may not come around often.

A trigger event that most people don't utilize is holidays. You can use any major holiday or even a Hallmark holiday as an excuse to send a warm follow-up. Here's where you can use social and lead research to see what people care most about.

Maybe they are an environmentalist and care deeply about Earth Day. Use that. Maybe they're a partier and have a trip planned to Cabo San Lucas on Cinco de Mayo. Use that. Maybe they're just a regular person and in that case, Halloween, Thanksgiving, Christmas, New Year's Day, Memorial Day, the Fourth of July, or Labor Day are all good reasons to wish someone well and follow up.

Also, if you know their birthday you can wish them a happy birthday, and you're well ahead of the game.

Make Sure to Follow Up

When you start to get responses, make sure to continue to follow up. Following up is super important and something many people are not on top of.

For tools to help with following up, try **Boomerang** or **Rebump.** These tools will allow you to preset e-mails to pop back into your inbox when you're ready to reply or follow up. You can also sync an e-mail to send at a later date. Some of the outbound sales automation tools provide you with e-mail plugins that do similar things.

I can't name names, but a successful founder friend would use Boomerang to trigger e-mails to send to investors at 3:00 am, so it would make it seem like he was always working super late.

If I tell someone by e-mail that I will ping him or her in a month, it's much easier for me to get that e-mail re-delivered 30 days later than to create a calendar note for myself.

Stitch App

Their new mobile product gives reps suggestions on how and when to follow up. It's built mainly for mobile, so it allows reps to make these simple account-nurturing actions on the go. Stitch allows you to take advantage of that time spent sitting on the bus to get real sales work done. They call this your Smart Sales Assistant and it connects to the Chrome browser and your CRM, e-mail client, and calendar for easy and smooth syncing.

Also check out **Immediately App**.

Reactivating Leads

Speaking of nurturing existing leads, there's one tool I really like for reactivating leads that might have slipped through the cracks or aren't getting the attention they deserve for one reason or another.

Datahug

Datahug adds value throughout the sales process by

1. Helping to identify high-value leads that aren't being pursued
2. Coaching the sales team with a Predictive Sales Coach that delivers the most effective next step for each of the deals in their pipeline
3. Enabling account managers and customer success managers to stay engaged with their customers after the initial deal closes.

Datahug first identifies the key drivers of your historical deals to pinpoint the magic formula for success so that they can feed these insights back to sales reps. Then reps can use Datahug in their weekly deal reviews to generate awareness and make it part of the process. Datahug creates lots of data that makes it easier to track ROI and highlight stale leads or pipeline that can be rekindled.

Featured Use Case:

Qlik, a Business Intelligence data visualization company, generated $6 million pipeline and $2 million new revenue last quarter by acting on alerts generated by Datahug highlighting accounts that had not been engaged by their sales team in over six months.

Datahug can surface the accounts that need action, it's up to you to take that action and make it count.

Chapter 11: Preparing For and Holding Your First Sales Call

Here's where you'll need to become less reliant on technology and trust more in yourself, your ability to sell, and your passion. This is where it helps to have experience.

For companies with large-sized deals, the first call you make is usually your discovery call. Others with smaller-sized deals can get right into things.

For example, if you're selling learning and development courseware for executives at General Electric, and it's going to cost the company $500,000, you're probably looking at a long sales cycle with many decision makers. In this case, your first call is about finding out a few key things. Ask questions, listen, take notes, diagnose, and then come back to prescribe.

Here are some questions to keep in mind:

- Are you in touch with the right person or a key decision-maker? If not, how do you get through to them?
- Do they have budget?
- How many people will use this product?
- What are they currently using, how was that purchased, and how long have they had it?
- What are the problems with the current software or process?
- What is the purchasing process like? Is there an RFP?
- How long do these decisions usually take?
- How many people are involved and who needs to sign off?

- What are their problems and how do they think you can help? The problems may not be what you assume and they may not fully understand what you do.

This topic alone can fill a book, so for more help with this check out *SPIN Selling*, *RSVPselling*, and Jill Konrath's books.

Again, the goal here is to set up another meeting with the right people. Set a time for that meeting while on the call. You don't want to pitch too much on this call, because you might not know what problem you're trying to solve yet.

If your deal size is small and your sales cycle is short there's no need for the first discovery call. You can get right into a demo or larger sell.

Getting and Staying Prepared

There are many smaller apps that provide nice little dossiers for reps that come right to the rep's inbox or phone before a meeting.

For mobile and on-the-go options, check out **Refresh.io** and **Charlie App**. Both of these apps give you fantastic prospect summaries to review before speaking to the prospect.

Things you might want to know are:
- Location
- Previous job history
- College or hometown
- Social media news
- Company information/recent news

- Competitors information/recent news
- Their social links and events they attend
- Their recent posts on their blog, LinkedIn, etc.
- Previous conversations

Maybe you share a common interest or know the same people from a previous or current job or location. Explore anything you can uncover that you can use to bond or facilitate the meeting. Again, don't be a stalker! Keep super personal things and accounts like Facebook and Instagram out of it. They don't need to know you saw the picture of them and their significant other frolicking on the beach in Aruba.

Charlie App

Charlie pulls information from hundreds of thousands of public sources, but one of its most important features is that your one-pager can be personalized by connecting your social networks. Once added, Charlie will tell you all the things your prospect and you share in common: whether it's people, sports teams, or hobbies. Each social media account you connect makes your one-pagers more personal, and helps you be more effective at building rapport. In fact, CEO Aaron Frazin believes Charlie saves an average of 57 Google searches per prospect.

Try using LinkedIn Premium with Charlie. Charlie automatically finds the person's LinkedIn profile and links to it in your pre-meeting research. Using the link to their LinkedIn profile, you can find additional background information after you use Charlie to dive deep into the articles they've been in, the things they like to talk about, and the breaking news on their company and competitors.

Refresh.io

Refresh is most helpful for the first or second conversation with a prospective or existing customer. The app creates a comprehensive online profile of the people you're meeting or calling, which prepares you to get the most from every conversation.

Just connect your calendar to Refresh and the app will automatically research the people you're meeting. Refresh will even send you a push notification a few minutes before your meeting reminding you to prepare; a full set of insights is then just one tap away. You can even set it to Auto Hide meetings with co-workers, so you're only shown external events.

Outside of this normal use case, Refresh is a powerful tool for maintaining relationships with high-touch and high-value prospects. As you get to know a lead or customer, Refresh ensures that you always have a reason to reach out and never forget important details.

Before getting on a call, always make sure you're prepared and know whom you're speaking to.

Now that you're prepared, it's time to hop on the phone with potential buyers.

Properly Qualifying the Prospect

There are many questions you might have to ask in order to properly qualify your prospects. To dramatically increase your chances of closing deal during that first call, you want to tap into the power of the past and the future. Here's how.

The Past

Ask your prospects about past experiences buying similar products or services and learn everything you can about their buying and decision making process. This is particularly useful for uncovering organizational biases for or against your type of product. If you're selling SaaS software and they bought something in that space three months ago and are super happy with it, your chances of getting a deal done will be significantly higher than if you're the first SaaS vendor they've ever talked to or if the last purchase in this space was a disaster.

Questions to Ask:
- When was the last time you bought something similar to our solution?
- What was that experience like?
- How long did it take?
- How many people did it involve?
- Was it ultimately a success?
- If so, why? If not, why not?

The Future

Once you've learned from the past, you'll want to focus on the future. This is what I call the virtual close. Ask the question "What would it take for you to become a customer of ours?" And then shut up and listen. Follow up on each answer and dig deeper until you arrive at a virtual close, "So if we did X and Y and Z, you would instantly buy, right?"

This process will educate you on the expected buying process as well as show you if there is real buying intent, and if there are any red flags or pitfalls you should be aware of *before* you start the sales process.

Questions to ask from Steli Efti, CEO of Close.io:
- What will it take for you to become customers?
- Once we've done XYZ, what happens next?

- Are we already in business or is there anything else that would need to happen?

Call Scripting

One thing in the past that's been hard to measure is how effective your call scripts are and the variation between reps delivering the scripts. I'm a big fan of creating a script for calls, but I will also allow reps to freely go off script when needed.

Scripts make it really easy to train new hires, which gives you a faster route to positive Return On Investment (ROI) on new SDRs, but that's not the only reason why I like them. I like them because scripts are something I can track, optimize, and measure. The main variables are the people on both sides of the phone.

Previously, you could only really track whether a script was good or bad. The rep was either good or bad as well. With the new technology era in sales, you can now track the entire script, as well as where people tend to fall off.

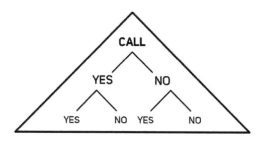

Call Navigator

If you have an SDR team that does calls and you want to track, measure, and optimize how your sales scripts are working check out Call Navigator. It's a brand new product still in beta, but boasts a solid user experience that allows you to flow through a sales script like a *Choose Your Own Adventure* book.

Call Navigator makes it easy for managers to write decision tree scripts and equally easy for reps to use the web dashboard for their calls.

CEO of Call Navigator Seth DeHart says,
> *Understanding the flow of cold calls and using the correct pitch path is critical to a rep's success. It is impossible to build true decision tree call scripts on a printed Word doc or an Excel sheet so we created an easier way for sales managers to build scripts that reps can follow.*

While Call Navigator is traditionally used to train new-hire cold calling reps with decision tree based call scripts, the SaaS dashboard is also used for building out pitches for new product lines as well A/B testing existing product pitches.

Featured Use Case:

Call Navigator was recently used by a sales manager who wanted to ensure his new hire SDR/BDRs ramped up quickly, generated revenue out of the gate, and had a solid foundation for cold calling.

Because the manager's reps were new to the company and industry and some were new to cold calling, he needed the reps to quickly understand the flow of prospecting cold calls, talk tracks, and pitches used to book demos.

The manager used Call Navigator and built decision tree scripts that his reps were able to use making live calls on their second day. Giving reps a solid understanding of how to call and pitch the product allowed the sales manager's team to have immediate success.

Again, I recommend you start with a script but trust your reps and allow them to improvise as they see fit.

When you do get on a call, take good notes and follow up immediately with a nice, neat, sharable version of your notes. Make sure to get the next call scheduled while on the phone. Follow up with an invite to that call and add a reminder in the summary e-mail. Also, make sure to end with action items.

For example, "Here's the information I need from you by the end of this week, before our next call.... Here's what I will have for you by tomorrow...." As I mentioned earlier, organization is one of the best assets that a salesperson can have. As your company grows, you'll need a better call system.

InsideSales

InsideSales provides you with a suite of tools for what they call Sales Acceleration. This hits on calls, voicemails, SMS, e-mail, fax, and more. I like them most for the features on their call products.

Coupled with your CRM, their platform allows you to prioritize lists to call based on predictive analytics and quickly dial inbound leads as soon as they come in. According to InsideSales, "A lead called within five minutes of requesting information is over 10 times more likely to answer and 4 times more likely to qualify."

They also allow one-click, pre-recorded voice messaging and the ability to call leads from a customized local phone number, which brings increased contact rates. The new mobile app allows you to call, record, and track on the go.

InsideSales also crosses over into a few other product categories like e-mail tracking, predictive lead scoring, and sales rep management.

Screw PINs and Access Codes

I hate PINs and Access codes, so I recommend using UberConference for conference calls.

Quick Tips in Sales Psychology

Now that you're getting on the phones, let's get you prepared psychologically. I wanted to share some interesting pieces of advice for running successful sales calls that are outside the norm.

The following is an excerpt from an article by my friend **Vanessa Van Edwards** who runs a behavior research lab and focuses on helping salespeople navigate behavioral cues. She calls it **Science of People**.

1. *Start with a Bang*

Always start with a bang. One study tried to figure out how to increase room service tips for waiters in hotels. They found there was a super easy thing waiters could do to increase their tips. All they had to do was start with a positive comment. When hotel guests opened their door, waiters said "good morning" and gave a positive weather forecast for the day. Just that one positive comment increased their tips by 27%!

How does this help you? Never start a sales meeting or pitch by talking about bad weather, traffic, or being busy. Always begin with a positive comment or anecdote. Great weather, fun weekend plans, or a favorite sports team winning a game. That gets you off onto the right foot.

2. *Don't Self-Sabotage*

The biggest self-sabotage mistake is to speak ill of a competitor. Research has found something called Spontaneous Trait Transference. They found that whenever you say bad things about someone else people can't help but put those same traits on you. The brain can't help but associate your gossip with you, even if logically we know you are talking about another person. If you say your competitor is low quality and unreliable, your potential client can't help but associate those traits with you. No matter what, when it comes to gossip, always say "no comment."

3. Use Awesome Labels

When you assign someone a positive label, like having high intelligence or being a good person, that actually cues them up to live up to that label. In one study about fundraising, the researchers told average donors that they were in fact among the highest donors. Can you guess what happened? Those donors then did in fact donate above average. We live up to our positive labels. When you are with a client or potential customer, give them genuinely good labels—I never want you to be fake or manipulative. So be sure to stick to positive truths. You can say, "You are one of our best customers" or "You're such a pleasure to do business with." In that way, they will actually want to be one of your best customers and try even harder to be a pleasure to do business with.

Now here are a few more from me:

Set the Agenda, Stay in Control

When I get on a call that I set up from a meeting, I always like to articulate an agenda for the call and then ask him or her if it is okay with them. This way, we can keep the call on track and accomplish what I want to accomplish, while at the same time making them feel in control of the conversation.

For example, "Well, I'm glad we're able to connect today. I'd love to go over XYZ and then would be happy to answer any questions you might have. How does that sound to you?"

Let the Passion Out

One thing to focus on is allowing your passion and excitement about the product to show in your pitch. Make it something they can be infected by. Reps should stand up and do calls in the main room. As the CEO of Mattermark Danielle Morrill calls it, "Speak loud and proud!" I myself like to pace around for all calls.

Also put an emphasis on inflection, especially on voicemails. John Marcus, CEO of Bedrock Data, describes this as putting make-up on your calls. By adding inflection to the right words, you sound more passionate and articulate and, in turn, more convincing.

Chapter 12: Navigating the Buying Process and Closing the Deal

There are tons of steps and actions that go into closing a deal. So congratulations on getting this far, but the reality is you're just getting started. Now, there's a lot of information out there on the strategy of navigating the buying process, which over the years hasn't changed all that much. Buying and procurement processes are still relatively similar year after year at the large, dinosaur-like corporations.

Before we get into the tools you'll need to better close deals, let's dive into some of the strategies from two people who are all-stars in the space and have worked on monster deals in the past. I'll tell you about more resources on this topic in Chapter 14.

John Barrows, leading sales trainer for some of the top B2B SaaS companies, provides us with top strategies on rules of negotiating, how to create equality in negotiations, and why you shouldn't jump to discounting.

Rules of Negotiating

1. *Rule of Reciprocity: People have a natural inclination to repay debts.*
2. *Conditioning: Nothing comes for free. Make sure to give and get.*
3. *Know what to ask and when.*
4. *Follow good protocol for pre- and post-conversation: Nail down a time prior to conversations and make sure all decision makers are able to join. Be sure to send summaries to follow.*

5. Objective Health Measurement: Stay aware of the health of your accounts so you know which ones need nurturing, and which are ready to close.
6. Time Management: Know what accounts to focus on first.
7. Common Language: Make sure you relate conversation to what you are working with.
8. Story time: Know what stories to share, and when it is appropriate.
9. Know when to walk away: Know when a deal has died and to walk away.

True negotiations are all about coming to a mutual agreement on something where both parties feel like they got something out of the deal. Contrary to popular belief, you don't "win" a negotiation by making the other person lose. Both parties need to give and get along the way. The more equal those gives and gets are, the healthier the relationship is and can become.

The problem in sales is that salespeople tend to be "givers." We give and give and give and expect one very large thing in the end as our "get" (i.e. signed contract), and we think we've earned it because we did everything they asked for. However, if we give throughout the process without getting much in return, we condition the client to treat us like a doormat. They end up having little respect for us towards the end which is why they either keep asking for things (discounts) or they just flat out disappear on us and don't even give us the courtesy of a call back. We need to find a way to create and condition equality from the start of the relationship.

Creating Equality in Negotiations

To create equality, most negotiations focus on a quid pro quo approach to getting things in return for what you're giving away, which is necessary sometimes but tends to lead to a more contentious relationship. There is something else that can be even more powerful to leverage which is a human condition called the Rule of Reciprocity. This rule effectively states that we (as humans) are all bound, even driven, to repay debts. We don't like owing anyone anything.

If someone asks us for something, the receiver actually feels obligated to give him or her something in return. The sooner we ask for something in return, the easier it is for us to get. By understanding all the gives and gets along the way and matching them up, we can know exactly what and when to be asking to move the deal through the pipeline to closure, or to get out before it's too late.

Don't Jump to Discounting

Often, people jump to discounting to speed up negotiations. Discounting has such a negative impact in so many ways that it's worth pointing out a few things to gain some perspective.

- *The average S&P 1000 company would suffer a 12.8% drop in profitability by giving a mere 1% discount assuming no increase in volume*
- *Salespeople make a bigger deal about price than buyers do (salespeople 8.3, buyer 6.9)*
- *Whoever feels the most pressure will make the most concessions*
- *Discounts kill credibility and create a negative perception of you and your solution*

- *Discounts set the stage for future discounts*

So what's the best way to combat discounting? There are some negotiation and objection handling techniques that can help, but the best way I've ever come across is quite simple, just have a big fat pipeline. The more legitimate, healthy deals we have in our pipeline the less desperate we are to close deals and the more confident we are in handling people who are trying to squeeze us. We can also work more along the lines of the client's buying cycle than our selling cycle. Too often we try and force a client into our buying cycle, which typically is driven by the end of the month or quarter. We all know Sales should be about the client and not about us, so we need to do what we can to get them to buy when they're ready to buy, not when we're ready to sell.

This is why prospecting on a regular basis, even month- or quarter-end, is so critical. Spend 30 minutes a day prospecting in some way shape or form. It can be cold calls, direct e-mails, searching through LinkedIn, asking for referrals, whatever, just do it. If you're sick of feeling cheap and using discounts to close all your deals, then prospect every day to have a consistently full pipeline and see what happens to your confidence and abilities to deal with discounting.

Objection Handling

The best reps have gone through every possible objection to every question ahead of time and have already built out the answers. That's why they never get caught in an objection.

Matt Cameron was the Global Head of Corporate Sales at Yammer before and after the multi-billion dollar acquisition by Microsoft. Before Yammer, he worked his way up closing big deals running Asia/Pacific territories for Salesforce.

Matt compares the objection process to jiu-jitsu and, more specifically, to an arm bar. When Matt was asked how one breaks an arm bar his reply was simply, "Don't get in that position in the first place."

The deal cycle is the same way. If you start by aligning your goals with your buyer's goals, you won't get stuck with common objections or roadblocks down the road. Set common goals and timelines from the beginning and do the best you can to hold your champion accountable.

After 20 years in the sales game, Matt has found that the most common objections are really only caused by two things:

1. You haven't sold value (to the individual, not the company)
2. Funds are not forthcoming, because you haven't sold to the person with the ability to reallocate budgets.

When he's reviewing an opportunity with a senior sales-professional, he looks for the key hygiene elements as follows:

- Access and credibility with executives who have the ability to reallocate budget

- A business case that describes quantifiable, time-bound return on investment with an emphasis on solution features that differentiate us from the competition
- An articulation of how the solution will contribute to the decision-maker's personal agenda

In conclusion, the best way to address the big objections is not to receive them in the first place, but if you do be forearmed with the antidote.

Matt also suggests using a push counter, which tracks how many times and for how long the customer has pushed the deal off. Deal stalls are the death of long cycle sales.

Demos, Proposals, and Collateral

Demo and presentation software is a hot area of development right now and I, for one, am glad to see it. I despise demo tools that make you download anything and I won't list them in this book. It's 2015—get it together.

A great demo is more than just what you put together. The software behind it gives the customer a good user experience and they remember and appreciate that.

Whether you want to increase opportunities to sell and upsell, improve a customer's user experience, or just engage with online customers on a regular basis, a good demo solution can increase both your chances of success and customer satisfaction.

On a basic level, there are a few things to remember when presenting.

- Create a demo that is short and to the point.
- Don't make them do too much to get started and be considerate of their time.
- Go slow and don't talk too much.
- Ask questions like, what are your thoughts on this? Does this make sense to you? Does this interest you?
- Take good notes on their comments and feedback.
- Always look for ways to get better.

Most salespeople still tend to use **GoToMeeting** or **Join.me**, but my new favorite is a company called Glance.net.

Glance.net

Glance Panorama provides a real-time, interactive view of content regardless of where it resides. Their extremely lightweight solution allows you to present within a browser, in the cloud, on a desktop, or on a mobile device. It's been the best demo software I've seen for getting a mobile demo. Best of all, I didn't need to download anything to see it.

You can use Glance to screenshare, co-browse, showcase a mobile app, see the other person, or seamlessly capture data.

Glance Panorama integrates with Salesforce.com, Genesys, LiveOps, Oracle, Zendesk, and more to provide co-browsing, screen sharing, and agent video, as well as capture session data for dashboards and analysis.

They also provide a personal use/SMB option called Glance Lite if you don't need the Enterprise version.

ClearSlide

ClearSlide labels itself as a Sales Engagement Platform that allows reps to get insights on how customers engage with their content over e-mail, phone, and in-person.

While they do e-mail tracking, screensharing, and content management, the main feature I like is their presentations and proposals tracking product. Reps can get a good read on what content is being digested, when, and by whom. Having this kind of visibility allows them to test and optimize the content they share with customers as well as reach out when the time is right, with the right context.

The rep can follow up with context and knows what points to hit on based on where the customer spends their time within the content.

They integrate with many of the top CRMs, CMSs, and e-mail services.

TinderBox

TinderBox is a cloud document manager for all sales collateral and aims to be your one stop shop from prospect, to proposal, to signature.

They integrate your CRM with your sales collateral to allow you to custom create proposals, presentations, or contracts based on internally approved assets. Then you can pass them along to potential customers and track and optimize the content as you go.

TinderBox tracks engagement on the content and notifies reps in real-time when actions are made on the customer side.

They also provide an e-signature solution for contracts sent through TinderBox.

DocSend

DocSend is the new kid on the block. They allow you to do similar things like track and optimize documents on-the-go and get information on what happens to the doc once it's in the customer's hands.

I really like their integration with Google, which is actually powered by Streak. It allows you to add content straight from an e-mail, without adding an attachment. This not only makes it easy, but also makes sure your e-mail doesn't backfire with an attachment that's too big or flagged by spam. You can control the links to the content you hand out and adjust who gets to see what.

For better proposals and tracking try **QuoteRoller**, **Quosal**, and **Qvidian**. For another easy demo option try **Meetings.io**.

For Sales Collateral, you can use either **Google Drive**, **Dropbox**, or **Box**. Drive is good to use at first, but as you get more users you'll likely need to upgrade to something better built to be a Content Management System (CMS). There's also **SpringCM** if you're looking for a place to put closed contracts.

You'll have to pay for these services, but if you have this much content and too many closed contracts to keep track of, you have what's called "champagne problems."

E-Signature Solutions

Sweet, you closed the deal! Now let's get them to sign quickly and smoothly.

A few good integrations to look for are e-mail client and CRM. These make it easy to get things signed fast. I use Google Docs integrations with contract all the time and it saves so much time. Make sure the one you chose is also extremely secure.

Here are a few e-signature companies that work well.

- **PandaDoc**: Really accurate tracking capabilities.
- **Nitro PDF:** Just developed new e-signature solution.
- **Echosign**: Robust offering with mobile, run by Adobe.
- **Docusign**: Works on any device and integrates well with Google Drive.
- **Hellosign**: Nice online user experience.

Asking for Referrals

The best time to ask for referrals is right after the deal closes. This is a honeymoon phase where both sides have entered into a new and exciting partnership, yet so many people forget this step.

When asking for a referral, or anything for that matter, be aware of the language you're using. Too often I see people asking for favors in a manner that presents it as, well…asking for favors. When I left Udemy I wrote my personal network asking people to introduce me to companies that needed a business development lead. I knew I wanted to stay at a small start-up, but I wanted to hear out all of my options and I didn't want to start hearing offers while I was still with the company.

One thing to know and never forget: it's not what you ask, it's how you ask. Instead of saying, "I just left my company. Do you know anyone who is hiring?" Say, "I just left my company. If you know anyone looking for a killer BD person, do them a favor and introduce them to me." It completely flips the script. Whether it is written or verbal communication, a lot can be said just in how you phrase things.

Visit HackingSales.com/Resources for more on nurturing leads and navigating the sales cycle.

Chapter 13: Bonus Sales Hacks

Now for a quick chapter on some Sales Hacks that didn't fit beautifully into any other chapters, but I thought were worth sharing.

E-mail Signature and Out Of Office Reply

For starters, too many people throw a bunch of images in their e-mail signatures. I don't care if it looks pretty, don't do it. Make your signature as simple as possible. The only thing you should add is a link to recent positive PR. If the title of the story isn't that good, but the article is awesome change the title in the link that you share.

Example Signature

[Name] | [Twitter Handle]
[Title], [Company name]
[Mobile/Skype] | [Office/Skype]

Forbes Names [Company Name] Top 10 Fastest Growing in 2015, Find Out Why!

Just link that to the Forbes article, even if it's just a slide in the Forbes article titled Top 10 Fastest Growing Companies of 2015.

If you're selling experts on signing up for Udemy, you can take an article titled, "Udemy Raises $32 Million to Democratize Education" and link it in your signature with the words "Udemy Raises $32 Million from Top Investors to Make Experts More Money."

Our friend **Scott Britton** does this with his blog to increase traffic.

Scott explains:

> *Instead of just linking my signature link to my blog, I link to each post individually following the precursor "Most Recent Thoughts." This not only ensures my link appears since it's a new and unseen link, but also provides more compelling copy that's likely to inspire a click.*

> ***What's the ROI on This?***

> *It took me 20 seconds to change the hyperlink in my e-mail signature within my Gmail settings. To measure the amount of traffic this drove, I used a **Bit.ly** link, which I reserved entirely for the hyperlink within the e-mail signature.*

> *It turns out that 45 people clicked on my "Most Recent Thoughts" link over the past 3 days. From those 45 clicks three people re-shared this content via twitter. Assuming an equal number of referrals per tweet, I used Google Analytics to project that this link was responsible for over 100 page views. Not too shabby for an extra 20 seconds of work.*

Another thing you can do it put your Out Of Office (OOO) reply to work for you. I see too many people with the generic, "I'm out of the office with limited access to Internet and will be back [date]. If it's urgent please contact [co-worker's name]."

How many e-mails do you get per day? I think I might get hundreds and this would be a key time for me to advertise.

Instead of a generic OOO, try something like this:

> I'm currently traveling with limited access to Internet and will be back [date].
>
> **In the meantime, check out our most recent article [company blog post, personal blog post, or recent good press].**
>
> If it's urgent, please contact [co-worker's name]."

This way you're not wasting those eyeballs you're getting while you're offline.

Mix in Some **Humor**

Sometimes adding a little humor can elicit a response. Some people like to go as far as adding funny GIFs or images to e-mails.

This can work well when a prospect is not responding to you or gives you a negative answer. One time when securing sponsorships for a charity event, I received a "no" from a company we had thought it was perfect for. I knew my audience, so I went for it. I sent over a picture of a really cute dog looking sad. It was exactly what we needed to get them to give it more serious thought. At the time I thought it was a reach. Now I'm not afraid to flex it.

People also like to do this in what they refer to as a break-up e-mail. Just don't overdo it, and know your audience.

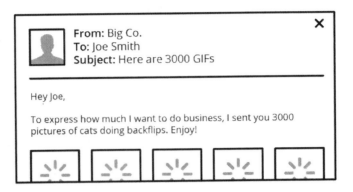

According to Craig Rosenberg, proven sales thought leader and CEO of Topo HQ,

> *Embedding GIFs in e-mails can work in certain contexts. It is important to focus on key areas like college, hobbies, puppies, etc. Note: this is best for social media managers, marketing, PR, etc. Don't send GIFs to digital security officers. Know your audience and use this method when appropriate.*

Also check out FunnyBizz for injecting humor into all of your sales collateral and operations.

Frenemies

Salespeople are almost always taught to connect with their prospects on LinkedIn. What they aren't taught is how to configure their privacy settings. Therefore, if you are connected to someone and they haven't fixed their settings, you can see when they have a new connection.

Now why am I telling you this? First go out and connect with reps at your competitor's companies. Most of them probably haven't played around with their settings and won't think anything of it when you ask to connect. Once you're connected, just wait to see whom they connect with. When they connect with a prospect, you'll be notified via news feed and you can send a very well-timed e-mail. Just don't mention how you knew to send them an e-mail at the perfect time.

Other Unique Solutions for Hacking Sales

MailLift

Go offline with MailLift. You might not have physical addresses for your accounts, but you should start collecting them. You really just need to know what office your target is in, and find the corporate address. Once you have that send them a letter using MailLift. MailLift allows you to send handwritten letters in bulk. You just supply them with a template, like you would in an e-mail campaign, and a list of contacts, and they'll write the letters and send them out. You'll have a lot less competition getting in front of someone in his or her physical inbox, and they'll appreciate the gesture. Almost nobody sends physical letters anymore, so you'll look good.

As a follow-up to this, I also recommend sending the main decision maker or champion a gift basket after a deal has been closed. This is only for deal sizes of a certain amount, but it will go along well when it comes time to re-sign or up-sell, and it starts the relationship on a good note.

When I was younger we had a business in which we sold real estate agents on running their social media for them. We started this business so that we could make American money while living abroad in Central America, which we did successfully. When we'd close a new account, we'd send the women flowers through 1800-FLOWERS and the men unique cookies. They would arrive almost instantly. Even though our deal sizes were $600 to $1,500, it was worth it to send $30 worth of fresh flowers or cookies to their offices.

What happened next was fascinating. Other real estate agents from that office would see the flowers or cookies arrive and inquire. They would then call us up and order a social media package for themselves.

Sending the flowers was a great way for us to indirectly advertise our services to the rest of the office—even if they probably would've paid us that much to send them flowers or cookies anyway. People like to feel special. Go the extra mile. Even after, especially after, the deal has closed.

Also check out **Postable** for handwritten notes.

Active Admin

Try out the Ruby on Rails App, Active Admin, as a way to track trials and uncover accounts to follow-up that are in the system. It's almost like a Dashboard-as-a-Service and it was designed for non-technical users, so anyone can get the most out of it. You can create a dashboard from Salesforce data, or your own server backend data that your Sales and Customer Success teams can easily sort through.

A shout out to ToutApp for showing me how they use it well within their organization.

Olark

Olark is a live chat tool that sits on your website and allows you to talk with inbound leads in real-time. This way you can knock out a lot of the discovery and needs assessment before they ever even get on a call. You can have Marketing Development or Sales Development Reps set up to take turns managing the chat and qualifying leads.

Or, create a team completely outsourced, either in the Philippines or locally (Phoenix, Austin, Omaha) to control the sales inquiries and pass them to your Account Executives, once they're ready.

Whoever figures out the on-page chat lead qualification system that cuts out the in-house MDR and outsources it completely, will have a massive unfair advantage. They can then take that saved budget and put it towards driving more inbound. This becomes infinitely scalable without needing more capital invested, and should drive tons of qualified leads to AEs.

I recommend testing it out if you think you have a service and team that can pull it off. Let me know how it goes!

Also check out **Zopim**, **LiveChat**, **LivePerson**, **BoldChat**, and **HelpFlow**.

Twilio

Twilio is an API that allows you to build custom voice and SMS solutions. You can choose to use this in your cadence by leaving customers generic voicemails or texts.

You can template these things. For example: "Hey it's [Name] from [Company]. I sent over an e-mail earlier regarding how we can help you with [product value]. Please [enter ask here]…

Sales From The Streets

For more tips and tricks from top sales professionals all over the world, check out the free app called Sales From The Streets created by John Barrows and friends. It brings the sales community together to share what's working and what isn't when closing deals.

Tips are broken down into categories that span every stage of the sales process along with other critical aspects of sales, like preparation and motivation. Since the video tips are all actionable and less than three minutes each, they can be used immediately for specific sales situations or digested during downtime, like while commuting to work or waiting in line for coffee.

You can also record your own videos and share them with others to help build your own personal brand and presence in the profession.

I always like to see salespeople helping salespeople.

Visit HackingSales.com/Bonus for more sales hacks that we couldn't fit in the book.

Chapter 14: The Wrap-Up

In this book I spanned the entire sales process from the salesperson's perspective and showcased over 100 tools for the modern salesperson.

1. You heard about figuring out your Ideal Customer Profile
2. You learned you how to find them and make the data yours
3. You went out and built lists of potential buyers
4. You found their contact information at scale
5. You learned different strategies for targeting prospects
6. You learned how to properly segment lists.
7. You learned how to look at the messaging process and how to track, measure, and optimize your outbound e-mails.
8. You learned about outsourcing and how to hire, train, and manage virtual assistants.
9. You heard about CRMs.
10. You found out the best ways to nurture leads and follow up.
11. You jumped into the process of preparing for your first call.
12. You heard about negotiations, objections, and closing the deal.
13. You found out how important it is to ask for referrals.
14. You uncovered some bonus sales hacks.
15. And now you are ready to put everything to good use.

I'll leave you with this: if you or your team embraces this new era in sales, you will be infinitely more effective than your competitors, and will leave them in the dust. You will win because distribution is king, and you *own* distribution at a repeatable and scalable level. Always be testing, measuring, and optimizing no matter how good the numbers are. You can almost always do better.

Again, this book and list of tools was created and curated for the sellers, not the managers. This is why we didn't dive into software geared towards sales team performance, hiring, and management like **Ambition**, **Rivarly**, **SalesHood, GetGuru, InsightSquared**, **Influitive**, **GoGoHire**, **Hired,** and so many others.

If you have ideas, success stories, or feedback I'd love to hear from you. Please be sure to tell me on Twitter @saleshackerconf or tweet to me personally at @maxalts. I'm always on the lookout for companies and individuals doing interesting things in sales.

If you'd like to share excerpts of this book, please make sure to credit Max Altschuler and Sales Hacker, Inc.

Visit us at HackingSales.com for more resources and bonus material on Sales Hacking.

Resources and Programs

Sales Hacker Programs

- Check out our content engine for top sales leaders and up and coming entrepreneurs at SalesHacker.com
- Get involved in a local Sales Hacker Series meetup near you. We're in 30 cities across the world and are looking to expand to as many as possible.
- Attend an upcoming Sales Hacker Conference to recruit, connect, and learn from the best.
- Check out our Sales Hacker Job Board for the best gigs in sales.
- Join the action in our Sales Hacker Community LinkedIn Group and start or engage in discussions with top sales leaders.
- Stay tuned for our upcoming Sales Hacker Veterans Training Program where we train War Vets to become Sales Development Reps
- Look out for our Angel List Sales Hacker Syndicate where we invest in and help build elite, early stage B2B SaaS Companies.
- Visit us at HackingSales.com for more resources and bonus material on Sales Hacking.

Suggested Reading for Sales Hackers

Publications
- SaaStr
- Bothsidesofthetable
- For Entrepreneurs
- TopoHQ

- Boron Letters
- A Sales Guy
- Heather R Morgan
- Matt Ellsworth
- Vanessa Van Edwards
- Mark Roberge
- Trish Bertuzzi
- Blogs of the companies listed in this book

Books
- Predictable Revenue
- Challenger Sale
- The Rule of Reciprocity
- Greatest Salesman in the World
- 42 Laws of Power
- Salesloft's TOP SECRET SDR Playbook
- Close.io's Startup Sales Guide

Sales Hacker Tool Box and Appendix

Tools Listed A-Z

About the Author

Max Altschuler is the CEO and founder of Sales Hacker, Inc. He's always been fascinated with sales, psychology, technology, and entrepreneurship, and considers himself an entrepreneur first, salesman second.

He was the first sales hire at Udemy, an online education company. He was the first sales hire and built the process that launched the instructor side of their marketplace. Udemy recently raised a $32 million dollar series C round of funding with a value in the hundreds of millions.

Max learned much of his sales hacking while onboarding experts and building out supply, with very few resources.

He's replicated this model as the VP of Business Development at AttorneyFee, which was later, sold to LegalZoom and now operates as LegalZoom Local. He's worked with many SaaS, marketplace, and ad tech companies along the way and truly loves finding new ways to help salespeople become more efficient.

Max started Sales Hacker, Inc. to help other start-ups with fewer resources sell their products and services to large corporations.

Max has a Bachelor's Degree in Interdisciplinary Studies from Arizona State University. He is originally from Syosset, New York and currently resides in San Francisco, when he's not traveling to help people hack sales. He's visited over seventy countries and counting.

To get Max speaking at your event or contributing to content, contact: getmax@saleshacker.com
For other inquires about Sales Hacker events or opportunities, contact: **marketing@saleshacker.com**
Follow Max on Twitter at @maxalts
Connect with him on LinkedIn at
www.linkedin.com/in/maxaltschuler

Acknowledgements

Special thanks to the people who helped with this book.

To my dad, David Altschuler, who held me accountable for writing this book while I traveled in Bali. To my mom, Karen Altschuler, who probably doesn't understand a word of this book, but supports me in whatever I decide to do with my life.

The original Sales Hacker group: Zander Ford, Ryan Buckley, Tawheed Kader, and Matt Ellsworth, who were all, in one way or another, instrumental in helping me launch Sales Hacker.

The guys who frequently came together for the early meet-ups: Zack Sinclair, J. Scott Zimmerman, Ilya Lichtenstein, Travis Wallis, Brian Kelly, Justin Mares, David Nihill, Jason Lemkin, and others.

To my contributors: Matt Cameron, Daniel Barber, John Barrows, Craig Rosenberg, Emmanuelle Skala, Aaron Ross, John Marcus, Scott Britton, Kyle Porter, Heather R. Morgan, Jorge Soto, J. Ryan Williams, Steli Efti, Jeff Hoffman, Vanessa Van Edwards, Farlan Dowell, Mark Roberge, Kevin Gaither, Ralph Barsi, Wade Foster, and many more.

To all of the founders and employees of the companies that spoke with me.

To Udemy for taking a chance on me.

To my Sales Hacker team that keeps the train moving.

And last but certainly not least, a big thanks to the Sales Hacker supporters over the past year—speakers, sponsors, attendees, readers, contributors, promoters, volunteers, and back-patters. You all rock and I hope Sales Hacker will continue to provide value in your lives and careers.

Please follow me @saleshackerconf and join the Sales Hacker Community.

A portion of the proceeds of this book's sales will go towards supporting the San Francisco-based charity, Muttville Senior Dog Rescue.

Made in the USA
San Bernardino, CA
17 March 2016